CHANGING WORLDS

CHANGING WORLDS

✦

Diary of a Jamaican-Canadian Experience

M. Evangeline Anderson

CHANGING WORLDS
DIARY OF A JAMAICAN-CANADIAN EXPERIENCE

iUniverse books may be ordered through booksellers or by contacting:

iUniverse
1663 Liberty Drive
Bloomington, IN 47403
www.iuniverse.com
1-800-Authors (1-800-288-4677)

Because of the dynamic nature of the Internet, any web addresses or links contained in this book may have changed since publication and may no longer be valid. The views expressed in this work are solely those of the author and do not necessarily reflect the views of the publisher, and the publisher hereby disclaims any responsibility for them.

All Scripture quotations, unless otherwise specified, are taken from the Holy Bible, New International Version®. Copyright © 1973, 1978, 1984 International Bible Society. All rights reserved throughout the world. Used by permission of International Bible Society.

ISBN: 978-0-5953-1817-9 (sc)
ISBN: 978-0-5957-6626-0 (e)

Printed in the United States of America.

iUniverse rev. date: 02/09/2015

Dedicated first to
my family,
& secondly, to
Christian Education
in Jamaica.

"Your kingdom come,
Your will be done
on earth
as it is
in heaven."

—Matthew 6:10, The Bible

Contents

Preface to the Second Edition

Ten years have passed since this "diary" was first published, and it has been a decade of great change. The world has changed, Canada has changed, and most importantly—Jamaica and my family have changed. It is the two latter changes that have motivated me to update *Changing Worlds*.

My first aim is to present biographical consistency between *Changing Worlds* and my subsequent writing. Pseudonyms were used for close family members in the 2004 *Changing Worlds* account. In the ensuing decade, my children have matured and granted permission for their real names to be used in my writing, acknowledging and giving God the glory for everything He has done in our lives. The substitution of their real names is the main feature of this second edition. That has also allowed for the use of my husband's first name, Michael, to replace "Spencer" which is actually his middle name.

The other important feature of this 2014 edition has to do with Jamaica. When Changing *Worlds* first chronicled our 1999 migration from Jamaica to Canada, it was already 2004. At that time, the Jamaican High Commissioner to Canada said my writing had alluded too negatively to conditions in Jamaica. I disagreed, but resolved to honestly correct any unpatriotic impression that may have been created, at the earliest opportunity.

The factual memories of Jamaica, land of our birth, which I committed to the journal in 1999 were absolutely true then. Furthermore, relating them was necessary to explain some of the culture shock and what I termed "deprivation therapy" that I first experienced in Canada. However, some positive changes have taken place in Jamaica over the years, so I have looked forward to updating *Changing Worlds* to reflect that, and to encourage the anticipation of more answered prayers for Jamaica. That is the other purpose of this second edition.

As a backdrop to other visible changes, it should be noted how foreign currency exchange rates have cumulatively affected Jamaica over the period. Simply put, in 1999 it cost $25 Jamaican to buy $1 Canadian. In September 2014 it cost $101 Jamaican to buy the same $1 Canadian. Given the far-reaching effects of this devaluation of Jamaican currency, it's a miracle that so many good developments have nevertheless taken place. It is also an undeniable credit to the spirit of patriotic, law-abiding, morally upright Jamaicans that so many of them have remained at home to persevere, under God, with their nation-building and national transformation efforts.

In Chapter 19 under the subheading "Finally…" some positive changes were mentioned as having already taken place in Jamaica between 1999 and 2004. These were the improved telephone services, public transportation, roads, and increased media representation of the distinctly Christian voice. These trends have continued, with communication technology and highway infrastructure following hard after North American patterns, and with the Church becoming more united and vocal in Christian activism on matters of national importance.

In Chapters 2, 3, 4, 5 and 18, I have added footnotes to highlight areas in which improvements have taken place in Jamaica. Notably, there is better customer service offered by many organizations, better policing and law enforcement in some locations, and more effective security at buildings such as banks. The educational system has also been improved, especially by equal access to different secondary education options, and the increased use of computer technology in classrooms and school administration.

The government and various non-governmental organizations have increased their efforts to mobilize the Jamaican Diaspora in developed countries to assist with nation-building in various ways. Rather than simply providing materially for their relatives in Jamaica, Diaspora members have been encouraged to combine and increase their efforts for the national good. Certain government agencies have been newly tasked with facilitating this, liaising with Diaspora representatives through international conferences and other means, and courting investment in Jamaica from Diaspora-related sources. This movement of "Jamaicans-helping-Jamaica" supplements in a welcome way the international aid that remains available.

At the same time, Jamaican athletes and other performers have achieved increasing prominence in international competition. Many have also upheld high ethical and patriotic standards in the limelight. This has positively impacted Jamaica's national self-image and, if psychological theories hold true, should auger well for the redirection of Jamaican youth who needed good role models to emulate.

Just before this manuscript update was submitted in October 2014, Jamaican media reported on an address by the Deputy Managing Director of the International Monetary Fund, Min Zhu, to community college students in the tourist hub of Montego Bay. Min Zhu reportedly said that Jamaica's achievements under the Extended Fund Facility Agreement could only be described as miraculous, and that the local economy is turning around due to the financial "miracle" that the Government has performed.

While the 1999 perspectives shared in *Changing Worlds: Diary of a Jamaican-Canadian Experience* still offer interesting historical commentary, the updates shared in this 2014 edition will attest to the tireless work of such organizations as the Jamaica House of Prayer and Operation Save Jamaica. Yet this new edition also acknowledges that God has not yet finished answering the prayer of our National Anthem: "Eternal Father, bless our land; guide us with thy mighty hand, keep us free from evil powers, be our light through countless hours. To our leaders, Great Defender, grant true wisdom from above. Justice, truth be ours forever—Jamaica, land we love!"

Acknowledgements

The cooperation, help, humility and faith of many people have made this book possible. I want to thank them for affording me the privilege of telling this story to bless others.

Whenever I write, I acknowledge the coaching of my late father, Clement, who taught me the basics of—and the love for—writing my thoughts down in an interesting way. He worked with me on essays throughout my childhood, and inspired me by his own devotion to writing. My mother, Cynthia, was the one who treasured, promoted and hoarded my earliest writing "successes"— little stories and poems that she deemed worthy of public scrutiny. I recall this fond indulgence with the deepest gratitude.

From the bottom of my heart I also thank my husband, Michael, and our children—Sean, Arianne, Gail, Deborah and Joseph—for their editing of content, their patience and their endorsement. I am especially grateful to Joe for his encouraging prophetic word, delivered in early 2002, regarding the success of this project.

The prayers, good wishes and advice of many Christian brothers and sisters, both in Jamaica and in Canada, have also helped me overcome the challenge of completing this book. I bless God for them. To Chief Cousin[1], the relative who facilitated not only our relocation to Canada, but also my pursuit of writing objectives and the foundational work on this manuscript, I owe a significant debt. May God grant him the satisfaction of having contributed to yet another, very successful project.

Finally, as by His own word "the last shall be first and the first last," I thank my God for the specific idea of writing this book—an idea He dropped on me in an instant as we flew over the Atlantic on September 11, 1999. May the product be to His praise and glory, and to the benefit of His kingdom.

Evangeline

---

1. Beginning here, pseudonyms are used throughout this book to protect the privacy of some individuals.

Foreword

No matter what the impetus to migrate, the decision is a wrenching one. In the case of Evangeline Anderson and her family it was particularly painful, for it meant family dislocations—with two children traveling with them to Canada, two older ones remaining in Jamaica and one already in the USA. Furthermore, they were leaving aging parents behind at a time when they would have preferred to be closer to them. The Andersons had gone to live several years ago in a mountain district that was remote from the capital, Kingston, not by virtue of miles but rather by poor communications attributable to difficulties with access. In this place they opened a school, raised their five children and communed with God, descending to their home church in Kingston for services on Sundays.

And yet, remote though they were from it, they were still subject to the pressures of the burgeoning city. And so, there came the time when, at the urgings of their children and with many prayers answered, they decided to emigrate to Canada in search of educational opportunities.

One early result of that trek northwards is this book, a set of reflections on the early days of a Jamaican immigrant in Canada's capital. The observant Evangeline, who began making notes of her surroundings and situations almost from day one, has credited a deficiency in her vision with strengthening her other senses and making her rely even more on things spiritual. This silver lining is resplendent in the pieces she has crafted. Even so, it is her gifted capacity as a writer and her innate sense of humour—which never strays too far from the surface—that have guided her thoughts, observations and reflections into print.

Ottawa is as different from Kingston, Jamaica, as first world is to third. Kingston is a bustling city in which the extremes of rampant poverty and lavish opulence are far more evident than in Ottawa. Then there is the music in Jamaica—present night and day, and the comfort of knowing with some certainty how you are going to interact with and be received by your fellow human being. Ottawa is spread out and its pace, by comparison, is somewhere between leisurely and lethargic. But in Ottawa the social services are dependable, the traffic moves, the buses run on time, a telephone can be installed in a matter of days. In short, there is a relaxed absence of the socio-economic pressures evident in Kingston, the progeny of urban drift, scarce benefits, scarcer jobs, and the resultant excessive reliance on extra-legal commerce that infest primary producer countries.

Even those whose anchor is their faith will have misgivings at the immigration process. You really don't know what you are getting into. However, simple conveniences like these that Evangeline found in Ottawa reduce significantly the angst and misgivings of those who cast out into the deep. For Evangeline and her family, migration has been a Shekinah light leading to a closer walk with God and a deeper understanding of His word and will. We are able to see not only Ottawa but also the tribulations of a new immigrant through her eyes. That she has put her actions and reflections in this book in her personal and personable way only strengthens her more... and the book, like a light that is set on a hill, has the effect of illumining all those who read it.

Ewart Walters
Ottawa, August 28, 2002.

Introduction

For my thirteenth birthday, Auntie D gave me a beautiful gilt-edged diary, complete with lock and key. It was tacit acknowledgment of the awesome significance of my new teenaged status, and she seemed the only adult on whom this had dawned. I loved her for it!

In treasured moments over perhaps a few months, I committed all sorts of thoughts, observations, dreams and expectations to the confidence of this book. Not veiled in cryptic verse like the thoughts Aunt Mona insightfully decoded from time to time, or my light-hearted, all-things-bright-and-beautiful word pictures like the ones Mummy took pride in; but in the plainest language possible, I just recorded unedited impressions.

Till the day that Anthony got his 12-year-old fingers on my key and opened my lock-box of soul secrets. What did he choose to do? Did he blackmail me to gain some tangible benefit for himself? I would gladly have paid. Did he, loving sibling that he was, give them back with the solemn promise never to reveal anything he had foolishly read? I wish!

The next time a certain boy came visiting with his parents, my dear brother took him aside and told him, *in my own words*, just how attractive I found him. The age of pushy girls had not yet dawned. I was mortified! Since the ground refused to open up and swallow me, I did survive the incident; but it put me off journalizing almost for good.

Thank God that age brought wisdom, a bit more discretion in committing thoughts to paper, and a bit more liberty in my application of the term "diary". The following chapters, which I have loosely called a diary, did begin as sketchy jottings made frequently enough between September 1999 and March 2000 to be a chronological record of those seven, eventful months of my life. But subsequently, sections were inserted to record my responses to current events, and some of these had originally been written as newspaper submissions. Also, excerpts from letters written home to Jamaica were included in an Appendix to echo the pathos of our experiences, 1999 to 2001. The names of some individuals mentioned in this account have been changed to protect their privacy.

Our family of four was numbered in Statistics Canada's count of 173,210 immigrants arriving in Canada between July 1, 1999 and June 30, 2000[1]. Some of our first impressions of Canada were later replaced by better informed ones, and various puzzling questions and observations were elucidated in time. These growing understandings had to be reflected without the luxury of continued journalizing, because after a while I no longer had the time. So, I worked some of them into the original as best I could, and added the rest in final chapters.

There was still the question of how much to include. Potentially, telling the whole truth could bring more useful information to more people who might walk a similar path at some time in their lives; but it could also meet with negative responses from certain others. If I sound like a coward you are not too far wrong. Let's just say I'm not the bravest person who ever lived. But rest assured, if this is not the whole truth, it's certainly *nothing but the truth*. May God bless it to your heart.

---

1.   Source: Statistics Canada's Internet Site, http://statcan.ca/english.Pgdb/People/Population/demo08.htm, August 12, 2002

Chapter 1

"Le Voyageur"

6,196 West Indian nationals emigrated to Canada between July 1, 1999 and June 30, 2000[1]

I'd like to coin the word "immigrantess," but it sounds both clumsy and politically backward. Pity—as it would aptly describe how I felt for the first few weeks that I lived in Canada. Much of life seemed surreal, like the earth beneath my feet that did not always feel solid. Even in learning that newly laid turf was a spongy cushion, letting me down easy toward terra firma, I was slowly coming to grips with living inside a picture that I only remembered having seen on screen.

When the glow of Toronto first came into view that early September evening in 1999, I had the twilight feeling that it wasn't really after eight. We were all terribly excited: my husband Mike, our teenagers Deb and Joe, and I. As we watched the brightly lit airport looming up to meet us, a rush had come to my spirit even before adrenaline got to the limbs, and I still think I heard God say, "Welcome to Canada."

Air Canada having delivered our money's worth, our family was wafted through Toronto Airport almost on angels' wings, in wide-eyed wonder at the sheer pleasantness of the experience. The contrast with similar passages through Miami airport was what struck me. I recalled the standing in long

---

1. Source: Statistics Canada's Internet Site, http://statcan.ca/english,Pgdb/People/Population/demo08.htm, August 12, 2002

queues, and the suspicious handling of Jamaican travellers by agents who demonstrated their assumptions of deceit.

Scary but Hilarious

Still smarting from the annoyance of having had my well packed luggage dug into by security officers as a parting indignity at Norman Manley airport, I could hardly believe that none of our 12 pieces was going to be searched. We were simply ushered into a lounge to await an interview. In great relief and excitement I joined my giggling daughter Deb, in her response to the events of this scary but hilarious day.

The scary moments had captured the tender goodbyes of one grandmother waving from her gate and the tears of the other spilling out at the airport. They included the final parting from friends who had been closer than brothers, and having to face again the unanswered question of how long we would be parted. Also scary was the rush from the departure lounge back to the security station in a bid to find Michael's hand luggage, discovered missing after the first boarding call.

Then, as we walked toward the gate, Deb's backpack had bobbed before me, its tag, "Le Voyageur," energizing the butterflies in my stomach. But the real gut-twister came a few minutes later as I watched the receding coastline of Jamaica, from which an umbilical cord seemed stretched as the aircraft took us higher, challenging its elastic reach.

The hilarious part had started with our being upgraded to first class in a kind effort to keep us all together rather than scattered throughout the rest of the fully booked plane. To the total embarrassment of my teenaged offspring, I usually promote myself as a blessed country bumpkin, having lived much of life in the Jamaican version of places my Toronto cousin calls "the boonies". This time, however, I behaved—and even tried to assume the air of a seasoned traveller. Only Michael in the next seat heard my whispered commentary as the unfamiliar, upscale pampering tickled me perfectly pink—or rather, darker brown.

While others watched the in-flight movie, the beauty of the heavens held me rapt. From a window seat, I matched the clouds to their textbook images and tried to recall all the classifications. I marvelled at the stately magnificence of the cumulonimbus, the delicate wispiness of the stratus, the unending blue that engulfed rather than overshadowed, and eventually the sweet rosiness of an expansive sunset. Then I slept—no surprise to anyone. I'm famous for nodding off, even without the sleep-deprivation we had suffered for the past couple of days.

Looking Back

Uncannily, all of that seems like ancient history now. The next few months also felt like the longest in my life. Handouts from a smiling Asian gentleman, who practically sang the welcoming brochures to us after we had left the immigration officer, are now at the bottom of a huge pile of paper, mainly decorated with red maple leaves. I'll get through reading them when my children have grown up and gone away.

The first journeys between Toronto and Ottawa stretched my understanding of space much more than visits to the United States ever did. With the constantly demanded response to automation and computerised processes, my country bumpkin self-concept first deepened, but has now been relegated to the trunk of skin-fits that aren't comfortable any more. Even my concept of daylight has been revamped, and my treasured cloak of day-versus-night activities has come apart at the seams.

While the Canadian climate can quickly bring on homesickness, some other inevitable comparisons were heartbreaking in the heightened awareness they brought of Jamaica's plight. Almost immediately I began a journal, with a view to sharing my first impressions of Canada with readers. These chapters are really the outcome of that.

For Third World nationals considering migration to Canada or other First World countries, this journal should help underscore the need for a completely new mindset. Those who have recently made the move should find comic relief from culture shock, especially if they can step outside of themselves and laugh with me at some of our common predicaments in these countries.

Others, who share a background similar to mine, will be reminded of the adverse conditions they left at home when they are tempted toward negativism—either by the new set of difficulties, or by the griping of new neighbors who know nothing but the lap of relative luxury. If you were a city dweller in your home country, you may not identify with some of my reactions, as certain things that were novelties to me might strike you as ordinary. Good for you! Have a good laugh anyway. The joke is on me.

First World readers looking through the eyes of this "immigrantess," may not only be amused, but also inspired with thankfulness for their taken-for-granted blessings, and overcome with an appreciation for the humanness of immigrants. Dare I also hope that Canadians will find, in my observations, a challenge to examine some of their pursuits?

Of course, I could not share freely without airing some of Jamaica's (and Canada's) dirty linen, and referring to business which is not entirely my own. This might raise the ire of those innocents associated with my shameless self, so I have used pseudonyms for certain individuals, and avoided any names except those which are public domain. I have also edited meticulously, reluctantly deleting some details.

So here you have it: the lightly censored diary of a Jamaican country-woman embarking on her first extended stay in the cold, First World country called Canada. And since I am what I am—an unapologetic Christian—readers will also find my journal flavoured with that particular salt.

Chapter 2

Sunday's Child

In 1999, the last census had numbered Ottawa's immigrant population at 161,885, of which 10,395 were from the Caribbean and Bermuda.[1]

When as a tiny tot I chimed the nursery rhyme "Sunday's child is full of grace," it had made me feel special, for Mummy said I was born at about 10 o'clock on a Sunday morning. Maturing reason had long erased that premise, but now, 45 years later it was Sunday morning again and here I was, starting a brand new life. Michael and I had arrived in Canada the night before, as landed immigrants with our last two offspring, the only ones still teenagers.

We had taken a rain check on the cousins' invitation to attend church, and slept late after coming in from the airport at 2 a.m. Then, in the light of mid-morning with the cousins off to their service, we took cautious peeks outside and made quick, exploratory excursions into our new environment.

A New Day

A new day had definitely dawned for us. The last time we'd lived on an avenue with neighbors in sight was over 15 years ago, before making that fateful move to the Blue Mountains of rural St. Andrew. True, the district had been blessed by our 12-year missionary work there, but this new scene held the promise of an extensive, long-anticipated furlough.

---

1.   Source: Statistics Canada's Internet Site, http://www.statcan.ca/english/Pgdb/ People/Population/demo40b.htm, August 12, 2002

I tried to take it all in frame by frame and sensation by sensation, marvelling at the contrasts God had engineered for us to enjoy. The first wasn't really a contrast to what we had left, but a contrast to what we had vaguely expected to find. That was the weather. It was quite comfortable—no cooler than we had left it at home before descending through the heat of Kingston to the airport. Now it seemed the popular horror stories of Ottawa's weather had masked any sensible consideration that it couldn't be really that bad in the second week of September.

Everything else was a real mouth-opener. We'd already been told about two high schools just down the road; but looking around, I found the proximity of other major conveniences to be striking. Directly across the road stood two strange, red and yellow structures, flanking what I recognised as a rather fancy mailbox. I discovered soon enough that these dispensed newspapers and—wonder of wonders—received and retained cash payments.

We would have had to drive for half an hour down our mountain, just to access the services these mute tin boxes provided. The district Post Office had been ten minutes walk from home, but I never dispatched mail there after discovering that it guaranteed a very slow and uncertain passage.

Were these newspaper dispensers made of some indestructible metal and secured to the ground by some unseen super-force, I wondered? And even now, in writing, my mind is warning, "Don't go there," as I try to find a cute way of describing the lights-camera-action scenes I had visualised, set on a Kingston[2] street suddenly blessed with the advent of attractive, money-containing machines. …Ahhhggg... let's leave that thought.

Disclaimer

Instead, I need to remind you what I said in Chapter 1 about airing Jamaica's dirty linen. I can't promise not to have a go at washing them, because I know that dirt *can* kill, even by just being in constant contact with you. Washing is what it takes to get them clean. So that's my intention in making contrasts—first to acknowledge dirt as dirt, then to separate dirt from worth in the wash tub of experience.

All housewives know that there are stages of clean—brighter whites and purer colors. Housewives of my generation and background also know that before the advent of chemical bleach, spreading out the second-lathered

---

2.   See "Preface to the Second Edition"

clothes in the sun took care of the bleaching. Then the washer would consider them ready to be finally rinsed, dried and returned to use. Likewise, I am determined to do some sunning, letting the light of new exposure shine on long-accepted discoloration, and trusting the sun-maker to work His wonders.

That disclaimer out of the way, I feel free to continue my commentary on the scene from the front door where I stood. Behind the boxes across the street was what seemed to me a most stately building, which we had been told was "housing for seniors"—in other words, an old folks' home. The sight of it brought a lump to my throat when I thought of the living conditions in which I had left my own mother, for want of an immediate alternative.

One of the things we had learnt through the months of data gathering was that Canada provides well for its senior citizens, but this was a concept I had never seen fleshed out in 45 years of living. Many old Jamaicans fend for themselves: the lucky ones with the help of relatives, but invariably without enough help from the government or other agencies.

Wonder of wonders again—just two steps east of the boxes was a very inviting bus stop. There was a time, aeons ago when I lived in Kingston as a child, that we had a bus stop right at our gate; but this was because we were living on a noisy, dusty, main road in a neighborhood that had seen better days.

I scrutinised the bus stop momentarily, admiring its almost-enclosing, see-through walls and the sturdy seating inside and outside. It seemed a delicate but elaborate enclosure for a bus shelter, and I noted that its counterpart was almost directly across from it, on my side of the road. This, however, was just an unsheltered seat on a large, paved rectangle next to a pole bearing a small sign on top.

"It's a... it's a... it's a church!"

With that observation my gaze crossed the road again to a building on the large corner lot east of the bus shelter. If I hadn't been told what it was I wouldn't have known; not only because its low sign faced the main road, but also because there was nothing in my experience to help me identify it as a church building. Its shape took me back to early art lessons on perspective: the boring text-book examples.

Later, I noticed that there was a cross adorning the architecture; but again, this was not conspicuous from the avenue. No problem—what really mattered was whether this building actually represented a house of lively stones or not. For the last 15 years we'd had to travel at least nine miles of rough, winding, mountain roads for satisfying Christian fellowship without the weight of leadership; so I felt excited at the very possibility of what this giant could signify. Around it, my imagination sketched the outline and fullness of a raindrop, and it fitted perfectly into the shower of blessings so far laid at my fingertips.

The cleanness of the street, verges and sidewalk were the last sight for sore eyes that I saved in my compare-and-contrast file that morning. Later, we were taken driving through Nepean to downtown Ottawa, Parliament Hill and Hull. We had our first lesson on local current events from my journalist cousin, and I feasted my eyes on gothic architecture amidst talk of the tensions involving Quebec, and the jealous stewardship over Nepean's city status.

Back at the house that would temporarily be home, we were using up every inch of space our hosts could generously make available. We were practically strangers to Chief Cousin's wife, Claire, but she had done everything to make us comfortable. They had room because their sons had all grown up and left home, though one lived nearby and another was bunking in the living room, on a holiday visit.

While overflowing with thanks for a place to eat, sleep and work as we tried to get settled in Canada, I stealthily looked around for a place to pray. This house seemed to be all wood instead of concrete walls and terrazzo floors like the one we had left. Almost every step sent a vibration rippling through it, and there seemed nowhere that early morning singing would not disturb the sleepers.

That posed a problem, because my personal devotions are definitely as necessary as good food and sleep; but they aren't usually very brief or very quiet, and they sometimes demand freedom of movement. Furthermore, as this working wife and mother in great demand, my private times with God seem possible only before the household awakes, rather than when we retire at nights, because by then I'm just too tired.

In our large, Jamaican country home it had been no trouble to find fairly sound-proof and shock-proof areas; and I explored this new house with the conviction that where there is a will there is also a way. Before long, I discovered the basement! (Rediscovered actually, as it had been part of our welcome tour.) Now I noted its concrete floor, peeping out around the edges of the carpet. Although the room overflowed with our relatives' half-a-century's worth of shelved possessions, I saw a large quadrangle of carpet that was almost enclosed by a couple of desks, two exercise machines and some boxes. Perfect; Sunday's child had come home.

Chapter 3

Back to School

In 1999, census figures numbered Ottawa's "external migrants" of five years and over at 37,195, in a total migrant population of 128,480.[1]

It was the first Monday morning of the rest of our lives, and we had a 9 o'clock appointment to get the kids registered in school. Still tripping over suitcases strewn across our two rooms at my cousin's home, we all got ready. I coaxed the others into declining a lift, so we could sample the walk we were proposing to have the kids do twice per day. We had seen the school on our Sunday evening drive, and it really was just a stretch of the legs away.

As we set off it seemed that jet lag, or nerves, or something was at work; but the brisk pace we had to maintain to ensure a punctual arrival helped me ignore the wispy annoyance that darted between us like airborne germs on a windy day. I was on cloud nine and refused to be summoned down. So, I can still recall peering determinedly in every outward direction, noting every detail that had failed to register when we drove past the day before.

I didn't acquiesce to the suggestion that we should take the shortest route across the grass once we got to the school on its open corner lot. The grass sprawled thickly across the level grounds in confident tenure. When I tried to analyse, later, why I hadn't wanted to trample it even in the footprints of the fast arriving students, I figured it had something to do with the school we had left in the St. Andrew hills.

---

1. Source: Statistics Canada's Internet Site, http://www.statcan.ca/english/Pgdb/People/Population/demo42f.htm, August 12, 2002

There, the notion of a grassy cover was absurd, even for a dreamer like me. Cut into a steep hillside, the schoolyard had remained un-surfaced; a dust bowl in the dry season and a muddy expanse in the rainy months. We had constantly battled erosion from the heavy rains, albeit with poor weapons, as there was no money to address the obvious need for retaining walls and impervious surfacing. Around us, the hillside farmers had an unreasoning disdain for grass. They kept their yards carefully free of it and sometimes sprayed the verges indiscriminately with weed killer—which was a pity, for they also suffered the effects of erosion.

Now, this lush expanse of grass seemed quite inviting, but at the same time protected by some invisible, hovering sensibility. So, I had not only declined to trample it, but stalled the unenthusiastic walkers as long as possible.

Never-never Land

Finally, we were at the entrance of the building—the first of these double-door entrances I was to march through fully awake. "There's outside, then never-never-land, then inside," spelt the keyboard in my brain. At home we just have outside and inside—and as many ways of making the twain meet as possible, in the interest of keeping cool without air-conditioning.

In 26 years' experience as a budding and maturing educator, I had entered First World schools only twice. The first time was in 1977, in Ohio, on a visit to my husband while he studied there. The buildings I entered then had brought the word "incarceration" to mind; but I know now that was an ignorant reaction, given their winters of which I had no experience.

Later, I had seen photographs of other First World schools—and what goes on there—from British colleagues, in the media, and most recently from my sophomore daughter in the United States. Some captured scenes to which I couldn't even relate. Others supplied visions of desirable facilities and adaptations, while some of the media clips just brought the gasp, "Whoa—let's pray we'll never get *there*!"

The second First World school I had visited was a kindergarten in Nashville, Tennessee, where I was given a guided tour by a colleague. On that occasion I was not representing my own interest, but soliciting material support for our mission school in Jamaica. The tour was brief as it wasn't a big school, but it had choked me up to compare their facilities with what we were able to offer our children. I saw this as no indictment against our own church community, just a great pity. In all fairness to my conscientious brethren, at any point in time you either have enough money to battle deprivation or you don't.

So, here we were now: through never-never-land, through the foyer, and inside a glass-enclosed general office. Before us at the counter was a very casually dressed student, apparently answering to a charge of late coming; and answer he certainly did. The exchange between him and the office staffer who was attempting to chide him went something like this.

"Why are you so late today?"

"I was doing so-and-so this morning."

"How could you have done so-and-so at the time you should have been getting to school?"

"Well, I did!"

Recognising this as a stage we don't necessarily want to get to in Jamaican education, I watched as he sauntered off and the unruffled lady behind the counter wrote something on his attendance record. Up next, we confirmed our appointment with the vice-principal, were given forms to fill out, and offered seats.

Forms are forms the world over—if you have filled out some you can fill out all, with a query here and there. Furthermore, after we had submitted their health and school records it was the kids who had to do the writing, so again I sneaked some observation into the procedure. By then, the immaculate appearance of the surroundings had registered, inviting a longer, closer look. Naw... still nothing anywhere that even vaguely resembled dirt. The freshness of the teenager forgotten, my rose-tinted lenses were re-focused.

Over the Counter

As we went through our preliminaries, everyone working behind the counter and flitting across the office was very friendly and polite. Not a grumpy or disinterested face in sight. I wished I could distil this quality, have it made into pills and send a shipment back home for our Ministry of Education to distribute, starting among its own staff.[2]

Admission applications completed, we were advised of a requirement of $25 per child for materials; but that was lost in the whole process of checking the documents,

---

2.   See "Preface to the Second Edition"

and no-one reminded us about it. We were ushered into an airy, private office by the vice-principal, who could have been the inspiration for smiley faces and the queen of ice-breaking small talk. Wouldn't you know, in the seconds it took to get us settled I was comparing her with a stuffy, ungracious counterpart I had dealt with in the previous year of the children's schooling. To be sure, that home-girl did not typify Jamaican high school vice-principals, but her stance as student-adversary and her unhelpful attitude toward parents did the reputation of the profession no good.

I soon relaxed, with the realisation that this lady's aim was to inform us about the school and its offerings, rather than to screen us for acceptance. Although the semester was in its ninth day, there was apparently no shortage of space, and we were in. So she proceeded casually through what seemed a comprehensive description of what we should expect at that school. Much of it, she said, was also outlined in the school's course calendar, of which she gave us two copies. We queried the points that were culturally unfamiliar and received thoughtful answers, while the kids were put at ease with an invitation to address her by a diminutive, which she said other students had coined.

Career Counselling, Anyone?

The next stop was the counselling department, to which the vice-principal escorted us to await the guidance counsellor. The latter would work out equivalencies between the children's Jamaican school records and the Ontario system, to recommend suitable placement for courses. In this room were comfortable chairs set around circular tables and flanked on one side by a wall of bookshelves and magazine racks. A busy staffer manned a reception desk while apparently overseeing the use of the room. We were asked to read the pertinent pages of the course calendar while we waited, and fill out more forms indicating our course preferences.

Having been forewarned by Chief Cousin to resist devaluation of the educational standard our children had achieved, Mike and I read carefully, but reserved the completion of the forms till we could have some key questions answered. When the guidance counsellor arrived, she made us all comfortable in her office, where we spent a surprising length of time interacting with herself and her computer—discussing and recording the kids' past courses, their career objectives, and the best pathways to University matriculation in a couple of years.

Where we were unsure of our conclusions because of scope and sequence differences between educational systems, the counsellor invited feedback within a couple of weeks, which could allow for modification of the choices. The only thing that made me uneasy was the uninvited emphasis I felt being placed on getting the children into gym courses and competitive sports. A coach had crossed our path while the vice-principal was taking us to the guidance office, and had immediately started recruiting them for various teams. Why did he assume they knew how to play these games? Was it that my non-athletic daughter looked otherwise to these people, or was it that all black people were supposed to be athletic? Did they encourage all high school seniors toward so much sport, or were there assumptions about physical versus academic prowess?

I wondered if I might be imagining things, but resolved not to ignore the advice of others who had walked this way before and warned me of pitfalls. My mother is an eternal optimist; however, life after Mom had not only pointed up the limitations of this outlook, but shown that it's often a cop-out to avoid examining issues and facing reality squarely. I know she would have chided me, "Shame on you for thinking such thoughts!" It would seem to her that I undervalued her memories of throwing discus for Jamaica in the 1940s, and being promoted from generalist classroom teaching to what became her beloved career—travelling the island as an Education Officer for Physical Education. (Sorry, Mom. Perhaps I still have a chip on the shoulder about being *your* least athletic offspring. Always felt safer with books!)

Whose then was the final word? It had to be Big Daddy's (God's), dictated in one of Paul's letters[3]: "Let us stop passing judgement on one another. Instead, make up your mind not to put any stumbling block or obstacle in (another's) way." Selah.

---

3.   Romans 14:13

Chapter 4

Is This Where It's At?

Census figures in 1999 showed that among Toronto's "in-migrant" population of 514,825 aged five years and over, more than half (337,540) were "external migrants"—not just from other provinces, but other countries.[1]

So here we were, at September 13, 1999. The last few months of our lives had held the greatest uncertainties we'd ever had to live through. Our whole family had felt almost blind-folded, and I for one had longed to rip off the cloth. It was like a nightmare about driving without my glasses. The only thing I could tell was that we were in forward motion, and the signposts were all blurred until we got very close—almost too close to give a signal.

Even three months before, the only certainty was that three of us were moving to Canada: Deb, Joe and I. Mike would accompany us at first, return home for a few months, and then rejoin us for good. The older trio of our brood had been on their way out of the nest anyway, making exploratory flights and testing their wings, but so far returning home like doves to the Ark. Now it seemed that a hand from the sky had reached down to remove the brooding hen and the last couple of chicks. Was the intention to detach the very nest from its perch, demanding that the fledglings start gathering sticks, or would a new nest be built elsewhere? We weren't sure.

I wondered if people of other religions go through times like these. Do their gods ever require that they sit calmly veiled while transported to

---

1. Source: Statistics Canada's Internet Site, http://www.statcan.ca/english/Pgdb/ demo42_96f.htm, accessed April 18, 2004

God-alone-knows-where for God-alone-knows-how-long? I needed to know this—not seeking to jump ship, mind you—but just because this question never posed itself in *our* lives before. Of course, the flip side which I *had* seen in similar toss-ups, is that the privilege of this peculiarity is discovered either in-flight, on landing, or when ruffled feathers have settled enough for the question to be, "Now what?"

There were obvious steps to take while we awaited divine answers. By the second afternoon in Nepean, we'd had the children registered for school, and they were to start the next day. It was Monday, and Mike and I needed to get back to Toronto for an early Tuesday appointment at the Canadian headquarters of the company that employed him. There, he would pursue prospects of employment with the company's Canadian branches.

Sold on the Train

Our in-transit passage through Toronto airport had been pleasant, but neither of us had ever visited the city. Having to choose between the bus and the train, we somehow did not consider taking the bus, perhaps because of our experience of buses. Reservations in cheek, we were taken to the train station by a young cousin, one of the generation we had never met before. There we found that we had misunderstood the schedule and would have a fair wait. We also discovered the fare to be a lot more than we had anticipated, which led to the thought that we should indeed have taken the bus.

As I looked around though, the station seemed as much like an airport as the one where my sobbing mother-in-law had kissed us goodbye a world away. Even the tickets seemed elaborate. By now I was growing accustomed to structures that looked like glass and steel in airy partnership, but the novelty hadn't yet faded, so I admired the simple architecture. While we waited, we bought Burger King meals at the outlet there. Although I had to settle for a substitute to my Jamaican favorite, their fish-burger, I felt pleasantly entertained within this giant, well engineered bubble.

Only when we finally stepped outside the building, to board the train, did the scene conform to what I had expected of a train station. Once inside the Via Rail coach I was again surprised at the comfortable appointment of it. To my untrained eye it could very well have been the interior of a small aircraft; and when we had put our luggage away, I reclined my seat and sampled the reading material from the pouch in front of me. If this kind of experience is covered by the term "culture shock," then these parts should be renamed "deprivation therapy."

Mike and I relished the ensuing hours of private, daylight chatting time; the first in five days. We looked at brochures of a college that offered helpful courses in computer applications, trying to plan my immersion in the tide of the 21st century. The opportunities seemed costly but limitless, and we bounced the possibilities off each other to see which could fly.

The smile I gave the steward when he first started to push his trolley down the aisle was more a startle reaction than anything else. Imagine refreshments being rolled down the middle of a train! Where had I been? Quickly scanning the fine print on the ticket, I discovered that no food was covered in its price, but that didn't matter as we had recently eaten the hamburgers.

The ride was uneventful except for pleasantries—not like the first time I had boarded a plane at Norman Manley Airport in 1977, when a delivery truck had smashed into its wing as it prepared for take-off. Now, the scenes through this window told me there was hardly anything around to smash into. The earth hadn't run out of space and I wouldn't have to travel another mountain road for a while.

We got into Toronto after 8 p.m. and sat in the station, watching the doors intermittently for the entrance of yet another cousin—this time one I knew but had not seen in years. I remembered her giving me the first lessons in sewing my own clothes, and then emigrating so soon afterward that she probably never heard the story of me doggedly sewing my own wedding caftan.

With all that there was to look at, we missed her entrance; our eyes only met as hers scanned the lounge for us, and ours played hooky from the door. A couple of warm greetings later, we were outside at her car, getting in to the enthusiastic welcome of her elder sister, whom I had not seen for even more years.

"Tronno" or "Tranno"?

The lights of Toronto flashed by thick and fast, towering over us imperiously, with an occasional twinkle that softened the glare. It definitely seemed more spectacular than its name sounded when reduced by some Canadians to "Tronno" or Tranno".

The CN Tower was pointed out as the tallest building in the world, and we never thought to question its claim. We were to drop off the elder sister at her downtown home before driving to a suburb where would overnight with the other. But before parting company with us, Elder Sister threw in her solemn advice. "You're in Canada now. Don't try to live in Jamaica at the same time. It won't work. Otherwise, you'll be fine."

Neither sister was thrilled at our plan for the family to be split for a few months, and to hang on to Jamaican interests as long as possible. I noted the warning, but it brought disquiet; so I didn't dwell on it. The question still lingered as to which part of Canada would become our home, so we were intent on getting as much of a feel for Toronto as we could in this very short visit. Our considerations had only focused seriously on the province of Ontario. One cousin in Jamaica, whose wife was a native of southern Ontario, had highly recommended the Kitchener area, which he visited annually. Statistics Canada's 1996 census had recorded 11,695 external migrants in Kitchener, out of its migrant population of 53,225.[2] However, our real choices seemed narrowed to Ottawa and Toronto, because only there could we could rely on the buffering of resident relatives or friends.

We were driving through Toronto at night without a similar memory of downtown Ottawa, but the contrast with Nepean was striking. In Toronto I would definitely be subject to more electrifying culture shock than in Nepean, though I had heard the opposite about the weather differences. The darkened spectre of one upscale, urban, residential area we drove through, showed such insignificant separation between the houses that it reminded me of a judgement passed by my late uncle, on one of the first housing schemes built in Jamaica. They looked like matchboxes, he had declared. In the dark, these upscale homes *could* have been huge matchboxes, just turned on end rather than lying flat like the butts of my uncle's joke.

The next morning, I realized that they looked better in daylight, as many lovely details I had missed the night before became evident at the suburban address. When this Toronto cousin chauffeured us at peak hour across town to our corporate destination, I noticed the anxiety with which she navigated the teeming roadways. She muttered about deteriorating road courtesy, and her body language echoed tension. To me, the traffic seemed ten times more orderly than the thoroughfare at home; but here the stream of vehicles was more relentless, approaching hard and fast.

---

2.   Source: Statistics Canada's Internet Site, http://www.statcan.ca/english/Pgdb/ People/Population/demo42f.htm, August 12, 2002

You Live and Learn

During Mike's meeting, we ladies visited a large mall, and were in a store when I made a vague comment about needing to find a rest room sooner or later. This led to a quick lesson in the mandatory provisions that store operators make for their customers. Sure, they could make millions, but not at the expense of customers' comfort, dignity, or welfare. Wow—what a concept! Something else to distil and ship home[3], which would no doubt be received with mixed reactions in September, as merchants and consumers set the stage for the net passage of wealth from consumers to merchants at Christmas.

Then, it was my turn to get some business done, and we drove to Bloor Street East. I had noticed months ago that Bloor Street tended to recur in the addresses that Mike encountered as he surfed the websites of Canadian professional organisations. So, although it had dawned on me that this was a mighty long street, I had failed to extrapolate any generalisation about Canadian roadways.

We found the Ontario College of Teachers (OCT) at number 121, and parked nearby, getting out of the car before being given lesson number two in consumer rights. After having put her money into the parking metre, Toronto Cousin discovered that it was out of order. We watched as she went beyond expressing private disgust to scanning the street for a police officer. Sighting one on the other side, she crossed over, made her complaint against the parking metre, and received some instruction on how to retrieve her money. Then, she moved the car and parked elsewhere, in case some other cop would take the appearance of the metre as an indictment against her.

As we walked back to the building, I saw the first beggar I had noticed in Canada. A comparatively clean man sat cross-legged on the sidewalk with his back against a wall, and asked us for money in a rehearsed, lilting voice as we passed. Here indeed was a surprise: not just a beggar but a white one, and me his targeted benefactor. I would never have conjured that up in my wildest dreams. All this learning was upsetting my brainwaves; major sorting and reclassification were proving necessary.

Up in the OCT's offices, I inquired whether my transcripts had arrived, and they had. The statement of professional standing from Jamaica's Ministry of Education should arrive soon, I advised the helpful young man who was politely answering my questions. Then I sought confirmation about

---

3.   See "Preface to the Second Edition"

the other prerequisites for teacher certification, and demonstrated that I had almost everything on hand. Only two items were unaccounted for: the medical certificate (T.B. clearance) and the all-important Social Insurance Number, which we had heard would be issued about three weeks after landed application.

The young man conceded that a copy of the medical certificate commissioned by the Canadian High Commission in Jamaica would do, for he was able to find the doctor's name on his computer. I should have it faxed to me; and no, they would not accept the rest of my bulky submission pending the arrival of the two delayed items.

Mike was less accepting than I was, anxious for a different response to satisfy the bee in his bonnet that I could be licensed to teach without delay. The young man at the information counter kept a straight face as I returned to ask whether the 'phoned-in provisional Social Insurance Number, of which we had heard, would suffice to eliminate the three-week wait.

"No," he said, "I'm sorry, we need a photocopy of the card."

It was past lunch time, and our hostess decided we should sample Toronto's multiculturalism in a tangible way. She took us to a Greek restaurant, and treated us to a hearty meal of unfamiliar but tasty cuisine. Then we headed for her home, as the departure time of our train was fast approaching. However, Mike had been invited to another meeting the next morning, so we decided that I should return alone and he would follow the next afternoon.

At the train station in Ottawa several hours later, Deb came bouncing up to me with the grin that said all was well in her world. She had come with Chief Cousin to meet the train, seeming totally at ease with this newly discovered, rotund and jovial relative whom she called "Uncle." For me it had been a full day, and I was glad to just wind down quietly when we got home. To our Ottawa cousins Toronto was no Mecca; and the kids, after their first day of school, had more to tell than to ask. I listened with interest but heavy eyelids; and soon, very soon, all the experiences of the last four days had been reduced to a skein of dream-threads.

Chapter 5

SIN Number?

2002 census figures show Ontario to have the largest population growth in absolute numbers among the provinces, due to a high level of immigration; as more than one-half of Canada's immigrants arriving between 1996 and 2001 settled there.[1]

SIN Number? What an unfortunate abbreviation, I thought when I first heard it. It didn't pass my test as an acronym either, for I found that it spells out Social Insurance Number-Number, which wasn't anyone's intention. Furthermore, it had a certain 666 ring to it, which I could only have escaped if I'd lived without sin-consciousness and never been spooked by Bible eschatologists. The next thought was that my sins were so many I'd rather not have to consider them numbered, thank you. So, I had resolved to sound off-beat and call it the S. I. Number.

Mike and I were surprised at the pervasive importance attached to this number, though there had been a Taxpayer Registration Number recently imposed at home, without which one could hardly conduct any business with the Government. The system there hadn't quite reached the point of rendering the un-numbered unemployable, however, for that number still pertained mainly to taxes, some of which not all workers paid.

Neither should we have been irked by the constant demand for the S. I. Number. It seemed to entitle one to a comforting range of provisions woven into a "safety net," the inconspicuous mesh of which became luminous in the

---

1.   Statistics Canada's Internet Site, http://geodepot2.statcan.ca/Diss/Highlights/Page4/Page4_e.cfm, August 12, 2002

event of unemployment. ("Secondary unemployment" that is, to coin a phrase differentiating it from the first job-search period for new immigrants.) So, I tried to swallow the impatience when we anticipated the three-week wait after our applications were in, repeating as necessary to Mike—who was choking on it—my impression that we had to accept the temporary, frozen-accounts nature of life without this number.

New Household Acronyms

Then, there was the OHIP (Ontario Health Insurance Plan) application to be submitted as well, which would entitle us to benefits three months after our date of landing. Mike and I had been given all the necessary application forms in our welcome-to-Canada packet at the airport. Having duly completed them with the kids to the best of our understanding, we set off to fulfil these legal requirements the morning after Mike returned from Toronto.

We had been directed to the Ministry of Health office in downtown Ottawa, and the Human Resources Development Canada (HRDC) office at Lincoln Fields. First we got a ride to Albert Street with Chief Cousin on his way to work in Hull. Left at the Albert Street entrance to the Ministry of Health, we played the revolving doors, crossed the foyer, easily identified the ground floor OHIP office, and joined the reception queue. Observing other immigrants at various stations in the large service centre, I breathed thanksgiving that we had passed the stage of life to be travelling with baby bags, toting toddlers, or restraining young children. There were couples there with all their dependents except the family pets.

At the reception desk we were asked whether we wanted service in French or English. Then, having been sent to a particular clerk on the basis of our English preference, I was surprised when she responded to a telephone caller in fluent French while attending to us. So began our brief relationship with a not-so-young lady who gave us her name to expedite future visits, apparently prompted by the experience of immigrants going back and forth from the office in piecemeal completion of the application requirements.

First, she checked our completed forms and our passports with the stapled-in visas; then she explained that to complete the application process we also needed an official document that verified our present address. She said this could be a bank statement or utility bill, and when we returned with this last bit of paper, we should just ask for her by name to minimise delay.

A Real Phone at Home

This was not a major setback, though it was already Thursday. We had planned to get our own phone, and open a bank account before the weekend. So the next stop was the Rideau Centre, a nearby mall, which we had been told housed a Bell Canada service centre. Following directions from the OHIP clerk, we set off on the short walk to the mall. Circumnavigating work crews and heavy equipment at a dug-up intersection, we crossed over the Rideau Canal, found the mall, and soon the Bell office. Minutes later we had applied for a telephone, received assurance of its installation within two days, and were heading out, discussing options for Internet service.

This added a special bounce to my step, for I recalled our years of applications to the only telephone company then operating in Jamaica. These had been submitted in community batches from the Blue Mountain district less than an hour's drive away from their headquarters. The applicants had received only acknowledgements and vague, rumoured promises. Cellular phones, which most people could ill afford, and through which the phone company exacted maximum fees for minimum service, had to suffice.

Given the terrain, our atrocious fixed-unit service had sent some clients heading for particular hilltops overlooking the city, to make emergency calls from hand-held units. If you happened to have a fixed unit and it was not an exceptionally good day, out-going calls were often interrupted by cross talk, and incoming calls were often not received at all, with the callers being told that your unit was either out of service or out of range.

Then, there was the "cloning" of one's phone number by thieves, who succeeded without much apparent opposition by the company, in making calls at the expense of legitimate customers. So, these sad excuses for telephones very often *were* out of service, disconnected for the usage deposits having been exceeded by a few cents. This situation had limited our use of the phone to necessary business, emergencies, and those calls you were *sure* God would somehow pay for. Our teenagers had preferred to stay elsewhere in order to maintain contact with their friends, and only faith had countered my dread of needing the police or a medical consultation in a hurry.

So, as we retraced our steps along Albert Street and headed for the bus stop to which we had been directed, I mused that it only remained to be seen how quickly the Bell service would be installed, before my comparison was complete. We found the bus stop easily, for it was much larger than the one across from our new home, and even at mid-morning, full of waiting commuters.

"OC Transpo"

Our next destination was Lincoln Fields, specifically the HRDC office in a mall called the Lincoln Heights Galleria. The wait for a number 95 bus was a short one, but in those few minutes I opened a mental file on public transportation in Ottawa-Carleton. The glimpses into Canadian life afforded by subsequent excursions via OC Transpo will fill several pages. But on this first ride, I was not yet relaxed enough to notice anything except the bus itself, and those first impressions would read better as an introduction to another episode, rather than a tack-on here.

This historic Thursday was the day that the area map we had bought became inseparably attached to me. It marked the launch of the independent reconnaissance of the Ottawa-Carleton area that would occupy me for weeks to come. Mike seemed embarrassed when I drew out the map in full view of strangers. He perceived a danger in everyone knowing we were newcomers, but I anticipated nothing except goodwill.

I traced our route, looking from the map to the signs at each intersection, and trying to memorise the road names. The Sunday afternoon tour to which we were treated a day after our arrival had left impressions of grandeur, and even some area names, but no sense of which names belonged to which streets. Besides, I was sure I had not heard "Lincoln Fields."

Despite the uneasiness, it was a pleasant ride, for the 95 bus route took us along a parkway flanking the Ottawa River. I noted how much green, open space there was even within the city limits. No overpopulation here. At Lincoln Fields the bus reached a terminus, a sprawling station from which we had to use an overpass that seemed to change direction as it spanned the parkway, taking us closer to the Galleria. It was after we had trudged beyond the middle of the overpass that I stopped abruptly, put away the map and muttered an admission that I'd completely lost my bearings. Thereafter I traipsed meekly behind my husband, latching hopefully on to his claim that *he* understood where we were going.

Back on the ground, I caught on just as the large sign of the mall came into view. We found the HRDC office, submitted our S. I. Number applications, and collected a handful of pamphlets which were comforting until I realized they didn't apply to us before we had been employed. We *did* have to wait in line, and there *was* a hitch, for we hadn't applied on behalf of the kids; but the clerks at the counters were efficient, so the process was quick. The final referral was to a lady in a cubicle, and that interview was over before we realized it.

Then we were out of there, armed with forms for the kids to complete, the load of our own SIN lifted, and satisfied with the morning's effort.

September 16, 1999. That's what the Scotia bank slip says. I checked it weeks later to convince myself that we really had proceeded from the Albert Street OHIP office to the Rideau Centre Bell office, to the Lincoln Heights H.R.D.C. office, and then to the bank, all by early afternoon, and *travelling by bus*. Of course, a schedule like this should seem commonplace to Canadians. Personal efficiency is perhaps something they take for granted from their buoyant perch atop a supportive infrastructure.

But, to me it felt like time travel—as if I had passed through two mornings and not one. I wouldn't have tried this at home, for it wouldn't have worked. I may have succumbed to bus stop exhaustion, nerve-wracking noise, and stifled gut reactions to the behaviour of dangerous miscreants before completing my business. Of course, I would also have ended up sweaty, soiled, and in bronchospasm from dust—at best, managing to greet our cheerless public servants with a pained smile. Neither would it have been much easier by car, not only because of stand-still traffic, but because of the paid, job-secure inefficiency we would have faced behind some counter at every Government office.[2]

So, here we were in wonderland, off the number 86 in our new neighborhood before the bus continued east. Just across the road was the Scotia bank branch that had been recommended as the nearest to home. We pressed the walk button and stood expectantly at the intersection for a moment.

The Home Stretch

Instead of a spelt-out sign on the other side, a bright, upheld palm told us to stay put; then a humanoid beacon modelling the first brisk step signalled us to cross. I thought, "What an irony—icons in a land of literacy and words elsewhere to direct the unlearned. How the world turns." But again, it was largely an ignorant reaction. Before long, I realized how many immigrants there are in Canada who speak neither English nor French, and for whom icons are a universal language to communicate road safety.

Inside the bank, we came once more to the impasse of the unverified address and non-existent S. I. Number. It seemed that the most worrisome

---

2.   See "Preface to the Second Edition"

question was our identity, but our passports—which we had been carrying everywhere for days—did not suffice. Before the invisible guardian of red tape was satisfied, we had pulled out our Jamaican Scotiabank ATM cards and account numbers, our drivers' licenses and national ID cards, as well as Mike's company business cards. We had even made a telephone call for help, under the watchful eye of an ever-smiling clerk.

Finally, an account was opened with most of the $17,000 that the High Commission had mandated we bring to Canada; their estimate of six months' living costs for a family of four. This accomplished, we suddenly felt the pangs of lunch time past. Crossing the street again, we headed for a fast-food outlet, and time out. There, I began to form the opinion that Canadian fast-food is not any tastier than ours at home. In fact, it was rather bland; but my mental notes on the service and the prices began with: "That's better!"

Being adequately shod for walking, we soon pulled our sweaters on, and took the slowest way home. Along this major road that was relatively close to home, we looked for stores on which we could rely for household purchases until we either moved to a different area or bought a car, neither of which seemed imminent. This home stretch had every sort of business place you could think of, in a long series of malls and strip-malls that intersected with well kept avenues of houses, schools and convenience stores.

Some large department stores had already been pointed out by Chief Cousin, and I tried to fix their exact locations in my mind. We also noticed others, my eye being caught especially by a Christian bookstore and the mall nearest to our drive. We must have been quite engrossed in assimilating these sights at pedestrian pace, for the same walk has never again seemed so short.

Chapter 6

Jamaica, Jamaica

Jamaicans resident in Ontario numbered 100,325 in 1996, of which 19,125 had arrived between 1991 and April 1996. (Figures approximate, from a 20% sample.)[1]

It was Friday—six days since we had arrived in Canada. We decided to stay home and resume the necessary business on Monday. The kids had spent the hectic days adjusting to their new school life, while Mike and I pursued the legal ramifications of landed immigrant status. In Toronto he had even continued the job search begun a couple of months before we *arrived in Canada*. (As I write, it seems as if I am wearing out that phrase; but the word "migrated" sends shivers down my spine—it sounds so final!)

I am really deeply in love with my country, if you can believe it after all I've written before. You may have seen a print media advertisement that pictures our sad love affair. There stands this lady, shoulders squared but head weighed down on one side, stately but forlorn, adorned with jewellery from ears to fingers but battered, staring out through clear eyes set in a swollen, bruised face. Each piece of jewellery she wears is labelled "He loves me" and each darkened bruise, "He loves me not."

Like many victims of spousal abuse, die-hard patriots of countries like mine try to hide the bruises and display the gems, never wanting to give up the hope of requited love. In the spirit of John F Kennedy's famous words: "Ask not what your country can do for you, but what you can do for your country,"

---

1.   Source: Statistics Canada's Internet Site, http://www.statcan.ca/english/
     census96/nov4/table7.htm

we labour on, excusing the abuse that continues to reward the effort. It's a modifiable behaviour, we tell ourselves. It *can* be remedied with a program of therapy and long suffering TLC, if "hubby" will only step out of denial and accept intervention.

Of course, since that's what it takes, the beat usually goes on till the damage is irreparable. But sometimes, God—whether in answer to prayer or in unsolicited pity—pronounces, "Time out!" In a sequel made in heaven, the lover recovers in body and spirit, is strengthened in resolve, and armed to the teeth before she ventures back into the ring, to do battle not with the man but with the raging elements that move him.

That's why I hate the word "migration." It says to my compatriots that I have given up; and that's a lie. There is hardly any poetry I remember better from primary school days, than Sir Walter Scott's lines: "Breathes there the man with soul so dead / Who never to himself hath said / 'This is my own, my native land?' / Whose heart has ne'er within him burned / As home his footsteps he hath turned / From wandering on a foreign strand?..."

So, I consider my sojourn in Canada to be "time out," offering not only deprivation therapy, as I dubbed it in a previous chapter, but also a *choice* of environment and opportunities for our last two children. Only for their sakes had I rationalised the gut-wrenching prospect of leaving Jamaica for a season.

The Sharpening of Arrows

If a quiver actually holds five arrows, then Mike and I had produced the proverbial "quiver full,"[2] in two sets separated by a mere four years. At the ages of 31 and 30 respectively, just three months after our 10th anniversary, we had our last child and deliberately put an end to childbearing. Thereafter, we held God to His promise concerning the house He builds: "As arrows are in the hand of a mighty man, so are children of the youth. Happy is the man that hath his quiver full of them;"(Psalm 127: 1, 4, 5, King James Version).

Having financed our first, Sean, to his Bachelor's Degree, and our second, Arianne, to her Teachers' College Diploma in Jamaica, we had also dug deep into our pockets for 12 years to help sponsor the mission school for the community. Meanwhile, our third, Gail, had challenged us with her bold-hearted conviction that she should study abroad. Fortunately, conviction and boldness were not all she had going for her. By age 17 she had completed grade

---

2.   Psalm 127:5

13, gained years of experience on her school's Students' Council, served as a very proactive Head Girl, and proven that academic scholarships were within her reach. So, she worked for a year after passing the British "Advanced Level" exams in order to save money, to secure her best scores in the American SAT exams, and to win a scholarship for undergraduate studies abroad.

When Gail began to receive offers, she presented us with proposals like a young entrepreneur. It would cost us no more than we had prepared to spend at the local university, she demonstrated. With figures that pitted her savings and funding offers (comprised of scholarship grants, on-campus employment and university loans) against airfares, living expenses and incidentals, she drove her point home. But which parents in loving relationship with their teens would just jump at the opportunity to send them far away, out of reach?

The clincher was our observation that God was adding His blessing to her efforts at every step of the way. He and she seemed to have made a deal, so we mustered our own faith and humbly fell in line when she received the best offer. The projections that her four years abroad would cost us no more than we had prepared to spend locally, proved totally true. In fact, she earned additional scholarship funding for research trips home to Jamaica, a study period in Europe through a university exchange program, and even voice training.

In the very first semester, she gave us practice in using email; weaning me from the alternative she disdainfully labelled "snail mail." With our telephone situation in the hills, I had to type the letters, save them to disc and have Mike send them off from a computer in Kingston. When she wrote home about using an electron microscope, her locally graduated brother could hardly believe it. He had never so much as seen a real one. Also, the faculty and systems at her college catered so obviously to the wellbeing and success of students that it contrasted greatly with what we were experiencing in Jamaica's secondary and tertiary institutions.

"Baby" sister and brother were coming of age to worsening prospects for their own continuing education. Even good students were being forced to rely on expensive, private tutors to help them cover examination syllabuses. Otherwise, they tried to do it largely on their own. And all without much promise of satisfaction, for the local choice of undergraduate courses fell short of their aptitudes and interests. Besides that, the continuing deterioration of the island's economy meant increasing unemployment and job insecurity for many breadwinners. Mike felt that his prospect of providing adequately for our last two children was definitely on the line.

He had successfully operated a small business for years, till his partner became discouraged with socio-economic trends in Jamaica and migrated to the US. Shortly afterwards, the down-turn in the economy had made it impossible for him to operate profitably by purely honorable means, so he had returned to a management position with the third multi-national company he was to serve in this capacity. Now, even the future of this company's operation in Jamaica was uncertain.

Mike's mother often chided us about our propensity for self-sacrifice and what she called martyrdom. We hadn't thought of it that way, for we daily experienced the favor of God, who is no man's debtor. But gradually, it began to seem that if we continued trying to be God-parents to a whole community, Deb and Joe could be critically disadvantaged. We wanted to take a break at least long enough to secure for them the opportunities they needed. That included the opportunity to help finance their own schooling, which we had learnt was not universally difficult, and the opportunity to choose whether they would spend the rest of their lives battling the odds in Jamaica.

Beginning in the fall of 1998, information came to Mike through a series of "divine appointments"—chance meetings with practical strangers, in which casual conversation unveiled Canada as the country of choice. He realized that it was relatively open to immigration, so we contacted my maternal cousins in Toronto, and paternal cousins in Ottawa, to alert them to our thoughts. Most of what we heard from them was encouraging. Next, Mike began to research the requirements for successful application. This led to correspondence with professional bodies recommended by the Canadian High Commission in Kingston, to have his credentials assessed by them.

But it was not until March 17, 1999, that we finally submitted applications for permanent residence, despite Deb's tireless agitation as self-appointed Guardian of the Process. Sean, now engaged, was not interested in going anywhere. Neither was Arianne, now a Kindergarten teacher with an itch to move out on her own and live in the city. Absorbed with her studies in the U.S., and already missing the Jamaica she remembered, Gail wasn't eager to even think about living in Canada. So, although she was still a dependent, we knew she wouldn't be landing with us. The submission cost us $28,800 non-refundable Jamaican dollars, and for each additional over-18-year-old it would have cost $12,000 more.

Mike's file logs the official process: the April 23 invitation to a June 1 interview at the High Commission, the medical examinations, the obtaining of Police Certificates, and the similar but more elaborate processes that Gail had to go through in the US as a named dependent, though she wasn't landing with us. Not until September 9, having already paid over $100,000 in air fares, did we finally pay $50,700 in Right of Landing Fees to the Canadian High Commission.

My file logs our correspondence with the Canadian cousins. In an epistle dated May 25, I updated them on our current situation and sent recent family photos, for we had been out of touch for years. After describing the children they had never met, I wrote:

> *"I'd like Deborah to be able to enjoy the pursuit of knowledge, rather than to stop short of her dream destinations in dread of the journey. Also, I want Joseph to be lured by his own curiosity and gifting, to explore and find his niche in 21st century knowledge and technology, rather than to be forced prematurely into a pressurised bottle-neck that will spew him out, all squashed, in some uncertain direction. (Excuse the melodrama—I am most comfortable expressing myself this way because that's how I see things—graphically. Humour me, please.) All of the above was just to make us seem less like unknown, long-lost relatives..."*

Back to the Present

Now that you have some more background[3] to this story, I can pick up where we left off. It was Friday and the kids were already four days into a widening cone of choices. We looked forward to their talents being honed in this broader educational process. They would escape becoming scientists or "techies" who can't appreciate anything literary, arts graduates who take the physical for granted without being able to answer any of the what's, why's and how's of matter, or unfulfilled people who abandon their dreams to plod a narrowing lane of lucrative occupations. Then, we could indeed envision them as sharpened arrows in the hand of The Mighty One.

However, by the fourth day of school, testy differences between Ontario and Jamaican high school courses were becoming obvious. The sequence

---

3.   For more background of specifically Christian content, see Appendix (letter to Home Church affiliates in the US and UK, of September 27, 1999, 12:25 a.m.)

in which Math topics were covered had begun to pose problems, and the approach to English was more slanted toward Victorian literature than toward the mastery of English for everyday use. (I suppose if a nation cuts its teeth on English—or French, for that matter—then learning the mechanics of the language *would* give way before long to gaining an appreciation of its history as an art form.)

Geography seemed more like an applied science, and the semester system made its own unfamiliar demands. As an educator, I rejoiced at the broadening that the new approaches would commission; but for the moment, I had to mourn softly with those who mourned. Mike and I knew that joy would come in the morning, with a distinct advantage having been forged as the iron of both worlds sharpened each other, and cooled from their friction. In the meantime, I comforted and cajoled between giving what scholarly assistance I could, and Mike delivered the occasional "stiff upper lip" pep talk.

By this Friday morning, we were also feeling a strain from the dishevelment of our well organised domestic life, and it was time for me to take some time at home to make things more comfortable. While Mike continued his job search, I deliberately kept mine on hold. I have this handicap, you see, of not being able to concentrate well on several things at the same time. Many women lay claim to this ability, and while I admire them, they will have no competition from me. If I leave a pot on the stove in pursuit of some appealing diversion, it usually burns—for I have forgotten it!

The weekend brought an opportunity to shop for warmer clothes, and for some furniture to organise the space we had into working dormitories. We had decided to remain at Chief Cousin's house for at least three months. He took us to various stores, running his tour guide commentary that was finally beginning to ring bells and switch on lights in my head. He had really driven us to several different places in the past week, and Mike's responses rewarded him with more evidence of recall than mine did. I chose the back seat, where I doggedly reviewed the map and watched the street signs, tuning in only to useful bits of conversation, while I tried to fully install the new program of directions in my brain.

We returned from our Saturday shopping to find our phone installed within the promised 48 hours, which sealed my comparison of Bell service with that of the phone company back home. Then, Joe tried his hand at assembling the student desk and chest of drawers we had bought in boxes; and he did a perfect job. Without any more assistance than he could have had from a vice, he proved himself a fully graduated apprentice of his do-it-yourself father and older brother.

On Sunday, we began testing the area's church temperatures by attending one in downtown Ottawa. It turned out that this wasn't the fellowship for us; it was too cool. My throat, hands and feet returned home burdened with undelivered praise. We needed to find a fellowship where people "after David's heart"[4], would congregate to offer the Giver of Life all the returns they could muster, and then to receive from Him and each other what they couldn't receive on their own. So, we'd have to try the church across the street next Sunday.

---

4.   See Acts 13:22

Chapter 7

The Cold, Hard Facts

Up to 1996, Blacks numbered only 2% of Cana5da's total population, and 3.3% of Ontario's. However, this translates to 21.1% of the total "visible minority" population of Ontario.[1]

On Monday morning, Mike and I returned triumphantly to the OHIP office with the Scotiabank documents we had collected on Thursday, as proof of our address. Miss Patiently Smiling X insisted she had told us that it needed to have arrived in the mail. The logic in that still escapes me. Who would deposit their hard-earned money in the bank but submit the wrong home address? And what prevented a Bonnie and Clyde type from having their mail addressed to accomplices who would forward it by hand once received?

Perhaps there is a good answer. We gave them the benefit of the doubt—as if we had a choice—and resigned ourselves to leaving this thing hanging for a few weeks. Over the next two days we submitted the children's S. I. Number applications, took out three months' interim health insurance, bought and installed this computer system which I set about using to my heart's content, revised our résumés and started making calls. Mike responded to job listings while I explored the possibilities in neighborhood public schools.

During our visit with Toronto Cousin, who was a newly retired teacher, she had advised that I offer voluntary service at any school while awaiting certification from the Ontario College of Teachers (OCT). I grimaced inside

---

1. Adapted from Statistics Canada's Internet Site, http://www.ststcan.ca/english/ Pgdb/People/Population/demo40b.htm, August 12, 2002

at the thought of this; voluntary service had been the story of my life for over a decade. It was one thing offering it on the altars of my God and nation, but seemed quite another thing here.

Nevertheless, I began to call the schools, and was redirected to OCRI[2] Volunteers in Education program. I gave my particulars to an administrator who promised that any school which needed a volunteer would get back to me. Then, I investigated the Christian school network, as a source of employment not bound by Government staffing restrictions; but this was sparse in Ottawa. The only one I located nearby didn't need any teachers, and the second nearest seemed at least three bus rides away. So, I put that on the back burner for a while.

The cold, hard facts began to present themselves as we made more calls and heard more advice. The system was suspicious of our qualifications, disdainful of any but Canadian references, and ambivalent in its response to foreigners—even those offering skills noted in the press as being in short supply. Furthermore, the job market commonly demanded bilingualism and a breadth of computer experience that neither of us had. Mike had a good job in Jamaica which he had not yet relinquished, so he was really seeking to secure the promise of a post he could take up in a couple of months.

He had an interview with the Ottawa manager of the multi-national company that employed him in Jamaica. This manager anticipated that there would soon be an opening in Ottawa for him. However, he would be effectively demoted from a management position to a technical field position, with more than a 50% decrease in salary, even at the 25:1 (Jamaican: Canadian dollar) exchange rate. The offer would be confirmed at a later date. Meanwhile, Mike resolved to seek something more suited to his experience and capabilities.

However, I had prayed for a career change, and looked forward to pursuing it here. So, the initial effort to establish a relationship with the Ontario school system was just an attempt to "fulfil all righteousness,"[3] in acknowledgement of the fact that my timing could be wrong. I really longed to begin a makeover as an inspirational writer, so I pondered and tried to prioritise my options.

While I awaited the OCT's verdict, should I enrol somewhere for training in French and computer applications? This would improve my long-term job prospects. Or should I pursue the job-search immediately, in the interest of reversing the net outflow of finances as quickly as possible? Should I follow

---

2.   Ottawa Centre for Research and Innovation
3.   See Matthew 3:15

my heart's primary leading into the pursuit of writing qualifications or its secondary leading toward training in financial management? Or, should I just work through a process of elimination?

When personally unsure and unable to reach a consensus with well-meaning advisers, I usually proceed through a process of elimination, appealing to God to bring the hiding puzzle pieces into focus, and relegate the almost-but-not-quite-fitting ones to the packet where they belong. Unfortunately I haven't yet found a foolproof way of squashing my own gut feeling, nor do I think it something to be trusted implicitly. So, a shroud of quandary, impatience and frustration can haunt these times.

A Time For Every Purpose Under Heaven

In the midst of these efforts, we had to prepare for Mike's temporary return to Jamaica, where he would try to fit the remaining pieces of our lives into a smaller but acceptable picture, before his own extended stay in Canada. His imminent departure meant we had to snatch elusive breaks from the tyranny of the urgent, to salvage some personal time. As priest of the household, he anointed each of us with oil in prayer, for spiritual fortification and commissioning to the challenges of the days ahead. Even in the precious hours that followed, non-personal discussions intruded, among them the tasks of recruiting a new chairperson for the board of the mission school back home, and fulfilling obligations to our church, where he was an Elder.

Soon it was Thursday morning, and we left for the airport at break of day. We had never before been at the departure end of Ottawa Airport, and all we knew of the local carriers was Air Canada. So, the first minutes caught us queuing up at a counter of a slightly different name before the mistake became evident. After we had joined the right line and moved quickly through the check-in, we had a breakfast snack before proceeding to the gate.

There, with hot chocolate growing cold, we lingered. Mike's thoughts were evidently agreeing with God's pronouncement that it is not good for a man to be alone, and mine were observing with Solomon that there is a time for every purpose under heaven. In 25 years we had never been parted for more than six months. We spoke softly to each other of the trust we shared with New Testament writers that God would not give us more than we could bear; and before that comfort could wear away, we resolved not to drag out the sweet sorrow of this parting.

Wake Up! You Are Not at Home!

Before 1961, only 0.8% of all immigrants to Canada hailed from the Caribbean and Bermuda. The number rose to peak at 9.6% in 1980, and declined again to 5.5% by 1996.[4]

In the weeks that followed Mike's departure, I started job hunting, and preparing to set up house. Gradually I realized that there was a tough, "immigrant-resist" cap on the job market and financial institutions. Some graduate immigrants had to accept minimum wage employment because they lacked Canadian experience—even with credentials declared equivalent to similar Canadian qualifications, by the relevant authority after a lengthy process. Also, as we had noticed before, English-French bilingualism was a requirement for many Ottawa jobs. A second language I did have, but in keeping with Jamaica's history, it was Spanish, not French. And the only French lessons I could attend were offered full time during the day, so the bilingualism hurdle couldn't be approached just yet, if I really intended to get a job working regular hours.

I discovered that even after the SI Number barrier is passed, one should get a Canadian Driver's License in a hurry, despite the three month allowance for use of an international license. The Canadian license is often the identification asked for in business transactions. Also, you had to attack the job barrier from all angles, including employment agencies—one of which demanded $5,000 and a three year "professional development" contract with prospective clients. They didn't hold their breath waiting for me to sign up.

In the meanwhile, one had to have cash for purchases normally made through credit arrangements. Forget the assets you had elsewhere—they didn't exist for credit purposes till they touched down in a Canadian bank. Until you had everything in place, you had to "cut yu yeye pan"[5] the fantastic furniture and housing offers involving credit, unless you relished wild goose chases.

A well-meaning Jamaican grandmother told me, when we met at an Ottawa bus stop one day, "Everybody who come to dis country 'ave to go back to school, mi dear." But forget the public re-training opportunities you may

---

4.   Statistics Canada's Internet Site, http://www.statcan.ca/english/Pgdb/People/Population/demo25b.htm, August 12, 2002.

5.   Jamaican Creole meaning, in this context, "look away from"

have heard about. They are for people on Employment Insurance, to which you are not entitled till you have worked a certain length of time in Canada and lost your job under certain circumstances. You had better finance your own re-training if you need it.

The Catholic Immigration Centre was helpful, linking people to free job search workshops and the programs of other useful organisations. I attended a week-long workshop run by a non-Christian organization which shall remain nameless. A funny thing happened at my interview for this program, which is the reason I won't name the organization. I realized from the interviewer's responses that he had misunderstood something I had said, gathering that I had competence in a particular area in which I did not. So, I quickly corrected his impression, not ever wanting to be hired under false pretenses. Whereupon, the gentleman looked at me quizzically, and asked if I used to be a nun!

"You don't need to be so honest," he added.

Instinctively, I reached for the cross which had hung around my neck for so many years. Never a nun—and not even a Roman Catholic, as he could have surmised from contrasting my empty cross with a crucifix—but always wishing to make a statement for Christ, I had continued to wear it although it seemed less accepted here to be an overtly Christian lay person. After all, the Muslims wore their hejabs[6] all over Ottawa in silent testimony to their religion, so why should I leave my cross at home? Subtle hints had been tossed my way by well-wishers concerned about my job search, but I am stubborn about things like that. Anyway, this poor man was not saying that my cross was a problem—it was just my honesty. Whether he was joking, I was not sure; but I laughed.

Thereafter, the workshops were useful: instructors reviewed current preferences in résumé presentation, gave us practice in interview techniques, and tried to orient us to the culture of the Canadian job market. There was also a week-long course in Internet job search techniques, of which I took advantage.

It was all leading somewhere, but definitely not fast enough for my liking. For comfort, I kept writing this diary; but by mid October I was doing volunteer work for a few hours per week at a Nepean elementary school. I also tried my hand at free-lance writing and editing. Before the month was out, I had earned my first bit of Canadian income—$150 from a publishing

---

6.   Head covering worn by religious Muslim women and girls

company for consultation on a proposed publication. In November, I earned $200 from *The Ottawa Citizen*, in payment for an article they later decided not to use. Nevertheless, I was so proud of that second check that I photocopied it.

Realising that these drops in the bucket would not suffice, I accepted a straight commission job, selling advertisements part time for a community paper. This was much easier said than done, and very slow going—by bus and without much administrative support. But I learnt more of the geography of the area. My trusty map showed all the wear and tear that I felt as time wore on.

But the most unexpected thing was to wake up to the realisation that I had become Ms. Nobody (not even Mrs., as such personal information had to be deleted from my résumé). The Bible says[7] that a good reputation is better than silver or gold, but my good reputation was back in Jamaica, and I hadn't realized that it would be worthless here. At home, no one ever doubted my integrity, or the commitment to law abiding practice in which I had been drilled by my preacher's son, ex-cop Daddy. No one there doubted my hard-working nature and pursuit of competence. The Governor General's Award I won in 1992 for service to society had meant something there, even though it had never helped with the grocery shopping.

Here, it was tempting to think that a little more silver and gold, and a little less of that reputation, would have stood me in good stead at a time like this. But, perish the thought; let God be true and every man a liar[8]. If He who knows past, present and future says that a good reputation is better than bullion or its progeny of currency, then who should argue with His word?

---

7.   Proverbs 22:1
8.   Romans 3:4

Chapter 8

Rivers of Life

"He shall have dominion also from sea to sea, and from the river unto the ends of the earth."
Psalm 72:8, King James Version, the Bible,
adopted by the Fathers of Confederation, for the Dominion of Canada.

Earth's waterways hold a strange fascination for me, eliciting the ambivalence of a secret admirer who would rather keep her distance. Earlier in 1999, I fell in love at first sight with the Cumberland River in Tennessee. Now I was responding to the lure of the waterways in the Ottawa Valley. As we crossed paths repeatedly, my attention was drawn to their dark, quiet, almost encircling presence. Little did I know then, that Ontario (named from an Iroquois word meaning "the shining waters") has a quarter of all the available freshwater in the world.[1] Bound by the St. Lawrence River and Lake Ontario to the east; Lakes Erie, Huron and Superior to the south; and Hudson's and James Bay to the north, the province also shows up on a large enough map as a literal web of waterways.

The turbulent, blue Caribbean had held a similar fascination but inspired greater fear, as it washed up memories of being saved in childhood from a near-drowning. Who knows which came first—the fascination or the fear? Whichever it was, I found the lasting allure of natural waters to be their deepening beauty, and the latent power that lies below the surface mirror. The very sky sees her face in the ocean, while its shallows display the tan of sand

---

1.   Source: *Readers Digest Atlas of Canada*, 1995, p. 51

beneath. But the inspiration of awe really comes from its depths, which have a hue all their own, and a power that continually erupts toward the shallows to invite conquest by the stout-hearted.

Occasionally, the meandering waterways of Ottawa returned my stares with lack-lustre gloom, and faces roughened in places as if by a rash. I learnt that some were not natural waters, but parts of the Rideau Canal, dug by human hands over 160 years ago. Its quiet promise lay in the freezing over of winter, when it annually became the longest skating rink in the world. I was curious about the often encrusted appearance of the water's edge. Chief Cousin said it had borne investigation in the past, but there it gloated still, like stubborn acne.

Cisterns Too

Then, one day, I did a double take as we drove by a section where there was suddenly no water—just a surprisingly shallow channel which was bone dry. Chief Cousin explained that the canal was usually emptied before winter, and my reflections led back to a sermon I had once heard. It was about the contrasts between the river flowing from the sanctuary, described in Ezekiel 47, and the cisterns dug by the Israelites, mentioned in Jeremiah 2:13.

The first was fed by a spring under the temple, presumably of "living water" as described by Jeremiah in his preamble to the metaphor. The latter simply stored water taken from elsewhere. The former flowed with an apparently endless, fresh supply, widening and deepening as rivers do; while the latter were "broken," and could not hold water. I could see them revealed as shallow, empty shams like the flat-bottomed canal which now lay exposed.

This allegory had been fully played out in my experience before, but without the striking graphics. There is nothing new about man's religious creativity, which has been misdirected in various times and nations toward the challenge of replacing the Creator with a created substitute. So I fully expected, especially in a society touted for its multi-culturalism, to find more religious diversity than we had at home. The cisterns and spiritual rivers would surely be intertwined here as their physical counterparts appeared, one set superimposed on the other, almost in defiance of any "which came first" or "which is real" question.

A Question of Thirst

All this reflection downplayed the greatest use of fresh water to mankind: that is, to quench thirst. The threat of thirst is what really got me started on this muse about natural waters. It wasn't a threat of physical thirst, however, but worse—a threat of having to forego spiritual watering. During the first few weeks as landed immigrants in Ottawa, we had been introduced to three Christian congregations. Now, choices had to be made which would put our lives back in Kingdom order—that is, submission to a local fellowship of believers and its leadership. But there were a few surprises as I discovered more about church life in Canada.

The first thing that surprised me about Canada's religious character was something I should perhaps have known. How it escaped our notice in the months of reading about the country is not quite clear. This was the strongly Roman Catholic flavour of public life. In speaking with Canadians about the school system in the first few weeks, and moving through the non-governmental agencies which cater to immigrants, the Roman Catholic presence seemed much more interwoven into the social fabric than I had experienced it before. I learned before long, that property taxes included a "school tax" portion, which the provincial government assigned to either the public or the Catholic school system, depending on the stated preference of property owners. I also found that Canadian Protestants didn't have the reservations about Roman Catholicism that are common among fundamentalists at home. One senior immigrant told me that she had almost pretended to be Roman Catholic, in order to have her children attend a good school some years ago.

Another thing that surprised me was to be advised by a leader of a para-church organisation that I should avoid white Christians, because they share the society's low esteem of Blacks. This seemed a weird notion, because I had never felt threatened by white people. It was more cross-cultural issues than color which had created problems for me in relating to some Caucasians. I had, in fact, been so generally comfortable working with and hosting white expatriate teachers at the mission school, that some of my compatriots had accused me of favoring them. They were wrong about my motives. I just favored people who got the job done, got to work on time, didn't shirk responsibilities, or abuse leave privileges.

I found the notion of seeking out a "black church" just as abhorrent as the notion of there being a "white church." We were approaching the two-thousandth anniversary of Jesus Christ's first advent. Come on! What had people done with Galatians 3:28[2] and Revelation 7:9[3]—ripped them out? (I'm not being silly here.) Naturally, if or when I detected hostility or disdain among any group of people, I would try to find more amicable company, and perhaps tack them on to my prayer list. I just didn't think it Christian of me to prejudge people—not in the face of 1 Corinthians 13:7[4]—or to assume that better company necessarily meant people who looked just like me. I felt inclined to give Canadian Christians the benefit of the doubt.

Church # 1

The Sunday before Mike returned to Jamaica, we had all visited a church that reminded me of one I used to frequent in childhood, as the granddaughter and niece of its reverent gentlemen. In this Ottawa church of the same denomination, I was again surrounded by ancient structures that defined the service. But there was nothing like the ebullience of my grandfather and uncle to draw sparks out of it. If I had gone to a museum to gasp quietly at the grandeur of its artefacts, or to a classical concert to close my eyes to the balm of its music, I would perhaps have been satisfied.

However, the challenges of adult life had proven too complicated, and my demands of it too solemn, to be answered by graceful architecture and soothing music. Also, the force that had evoked vociferous preaching and pulpit thumping from my grandfather, now demanded response from my own mouth and hands and feet as well; response, not to the hushed tone of the minister, but to the Spirit who had called me here. This quiet sitting in audience style, and making only the prescribed, circumspect responses was definitely going to "quench the Spirit"[5] rather than the thirst.

---

2. "There is neither Jew nor Greek, male nor female, slave nor free, for you are all one in Christ Jesus."
3. "...there before me was a great multitude that no-one could count, from every nation, tribe, people and language, standing before the throne and in front of the Lamb..."
4. "(Love) always protects, always trusts, always hopes, always perseveres."
5. 1 Thessalonians 5:19

Church # 2

The first Sunday morning after Mike's departure, I left the children at home to spare them the vagrancies of our quest, and went to check out the church across the street. This one was of a different denomination, and here I had a number of pleasant surprises. First, the atmosphere was less staid, and the inflow of worshippers more free and cheerful. Secondly, the musicians on the platform functioned as worship *leaders* to a greater extent than simply performing as a choir. This invited and inspired more vigorous congregational participation, especially as they led not only in voice, but in some of the praise actions enjoined by both David and Paul of the Bible.

I breathed a sigh of relief as my eager hands were freed to either contribute to the rhythm of the worship, or simply hail the God of Heaven. Here they sang some worship songs I loved, which had not yet been used in the wide repertoire of my home church. Goody! Now they wouldn't be relegated only to personal devotions, and I could write to the Trinidadian mentor from whose tape I had learnt them, to tell her about this lovely development.

With dignified movements, these worship leaders even encouraged some gentle swaying and bobbing of bodies as we sang, and I could live with that. "Hinds' feet"[6] we definitely did not share, however; so, for the dancing and prancing about I'd just continue to offer that peculiar sacrifice in my basement sanctuary.

At offering time, I was handed what seemed an elaborate visitor's packet— much more posh than anything I had seen used for that purpose before. It impressed me with its schedule of opportunities for special-interest fellowship and small group interaction at various times in the week. This was more like it.

Another thing that impressed me was a printed request for wearers of perfume to avoid sitting in a certain section of the sanctuary, which was reserved for allergy sufferers. This was consistent with the institutionalised courtesy and acceptance of diversity that I had observed since arriving in Canada. I hushed my immediate questions of whether these allergy sufferers had been presented with the lifestyle options that offer relief from their affliction, or whether there was also an institutionalised acceptance of its tyranny.

---

6.   2 Samuel 22:34, Psalm 18:33, Habakkuk 3:19, King James Version

Instead, I allowed myself the wish that our Jamaican congregations would adopt a similarly considerate attitude toward members who wince at the rising decibels that titillate deafened youth. Who needs perfume or hard rock volume anyway, if it's going to distract others from the worship of God? Perhaps the hyper-sensitivity of some noses and ears is something for which God has good use, and not simply an aberration. Perhaps they even reflect, to some extent, a sensitivity to unwholesome stimuli which we have otherwise lost, having become inoculated by increasing doses of pollutants in our environment.

As I read the statement of faith in the visitor's brochure, there was nothing there to sound a caution. It declared a stand on the controversial issue of the pre-tribulation "rapture," which some theologians avoid because the arguments on both sides seem equally valid. But I could live with that too; it wasn't one of the "weightier matters of doctrine,"[7] and I secretly hoped that time would prove the "pre-trib" rapture theory true. The weightier matters revolve around the use of our time on earth, and not around daydreams of our exit; although I too know the value of a hope that causes present trials to pale in comparison.

Plurality of leadership also jumped at me from the brochure. Excellent! Who wanted to be part of a congregation that relegated the expansive mind of Christ to a one-man headship? While the senior pastor delivered the sermon, I noted his frequent reference to scripture, in tacit acknowledgement of the congregation's need to see for themselves, in the Bible, the words that would verify his assertions. That was another plus that I had missed at Church #1, where the minister's words had been like a rambling rose whose roots were not visible, let alone the structure that supported its meandering branches, or the tendrils that anchored them.

I went home thinking, "What could be easier than stepping across the street for fellowship on a Sunday, or any other day for that matter? And isn't God marvellous to move me from a place where 12 years of missionary work had meant the sacrifice of personal nurturing, to a place where all I have to do is step across the street for two opportunities on Sunday and at least one in the week?"

As I scanned the church's mid-week options at home, the paper seemed to whisper that God was truly no man's debtor, and neither was He any woman's. The ease of the whole situation continued to amaze me. It seemed uncanny.

---

7.   Matthew 23:23

Was this too easy? Was there some catch here? I chided myself that the austerity of the past years had actually made me suspicious of abundance, and decided, without any further ado, to sample options from the schedule that very week. No more of that today though. It had been a long morning, lunch was the urgency of the moment, and I wasn't in the mood for decision-making.[8]

---

8.   For more on Church # 2, and personal spirituality around this time, see Appendix (letter to Home Church Fellowship, of September 27, 1999, 9:33 a.m.)

Chapter 9

Streetwise

"A city of villages" is how The Ottawa Citizen described the new Ottawa, as the old Regional Municipality of Ottawa-Carleton, with eleven municipalities in its orbit, geared up for final transformation into the one city envisioned in 1791 by British Governor, Sir Guy Carleton. [1.]

Before long, the road system and its nomenclature were beginning to make sense. First, I had to delete words like "Road," "Avenue," "Street" and "Drive" from my oral address vocabulary. Even the telephone directory sometimes omitted these words. Only the actual street sign displayed at each intersection told you in English and French whether it was a road, street, avenue or drive. So, for all practical purposes, Merivale Road was just "Merivale" and Bank Street was just "Bank."

Another key was to think in terms of the compass—North, South, East and West. Not "up," "down," "right," "left" or "just around the corner," as we tended to direct each other in Jamaica. For example, one would be told, "Go east on Baseline, then north on Clyde."

The understanding of intersections was also critical for interpreting directions. An address could be described as being "at Kent and Laurier," meaning "near the intersection of Kent Street and Laurier Avenue." Similarly, you might be told, "It's on Albert, at Lyon," meaning "on Albert Street, but close to the intersection with Lyon Street."

---

1.   *The Ottawa Citizen*, November 30, 1999

Ottawa's French connection was reflected in many road names, even outside of Vanier and Orleans, two areas where the francophone population was concentrated. Many Blacks from Haiti, as well as other Caribbean and African French-speaking countries, have settled in bilingual Ottawa rather than in Montreal or other parts of French-speaking Quebec. So, pronunciation of street names was often a challenge for me, especially when following telephone directions. I was sometimes unable to match the phonetics to the spelling on the map and street signs.

Gradually, I learnt; but it still surprised me how differently various people pronounced, for example, "St. Laurent Boulevard." Another strange pronunciation that confused me at first, and for which I have found no explanation, was "Oglevie" for "O'gilvie." It reminded me of the way the villagers back home had produced "Merland" out of "Maryland."

Another peculiarity was that roads could change names at strange places, and sometimes pick up their old names a few kilometres away. As an example of the first instance, Baseline going east became "Heron" at Prince of Wales, and Meadowlands became "Hog's Back," also at Prince of Wales. Chief Cousin explained that Prince of Wales was the boundary between municipalities, so the roads had different names on either side.

Examples of the second complication were St. Laurent Boulevard and Russell Road. Russell going north seemed to end where it met St. Laurent going south, but that was not really the end of it. Some distance north of that point, Smythe Road met St. Laurent, and Russell resumed as an offshoot of Smythe. It was very confusing for newcomer commuting.

The numbering of high-rise business addresses also took some orientation, and at first I confused the street number with the suite number, when the word "suite" or its abbreviation did not appear in the address. The suite number was itself a composite of the floor number and the room number. That is, Ste.1645 meant "room 45 on the 16th floor," and 911—1464 Baseline Road meant "suite 11 on the 9th floor, at 1465 Baseline."

Intellectually, all that was easy to grasp, but as hard as I tried, the right-hand-drive traffic system was a most difficult adjustment to make. As a passenger, especially at large intersections, I sometimes panicked for an instant, thinking we were in the wrong lane. Exits off some roads were also confusing; that is, turning right to go left (via an underpass or overpass connecting to the road you could have accessed earlier by a left turn, were it not prohibited).

It Takes All Kinds

One day, I had crossed over to the western sidewalk of Bank Street and walked briskly to the bus stop, before realising that traffic was streaming south on my side of the road, while I needed to go north. Amused and slightly self-conscious, I made an exaggeratedly casual about-turn and headed back toward the pedestrian crossing, to retrace my steps to the bus stop I had hurriedly passed on the other side. It wasn't until I had crossed again and stepped onto the curb that the little old lady came into focus.

She was short, clean and seemed well fed. Carrying a hand bag on her left forearm, old lady style, she seemed comfortably dressed, but not stepping out of Grandma's Vogue Magazine. The fashion statement I only analysed in retrospect, following the nuances to which Mike had alerted me a few days before, in an effort to help me interpret what met the eye in Canada.

In this case, it wasn't that the unfamiliar surroundings had rendered me unobservant. It was my automatic receptivity to non-visual stimuli that was at work here, distracting my focus from the visual. The impaired vision which had gone uncorrected for most of my childhood had left me with the blessed advantage of heightened sensitivities, which continue to yield information the eyes can't.

Warming to this stranger, perhaps as my usual response to little old ladies, I remembered having seen her coming in the opposite direction the first time I crossed the road. I wondered why she was still standing there. Her skin had seen better days—but so has my mother's—and annoyance registered on her face as she shifted impatiently from one foot to another. I said a cheerful hello, and changed course slightly to avoid bumping into her, before stopping a couple of steps away. She didn't need a second word. It seems she had wanted someone to talk to, or perhaps just a pair of ears to tune in to her complaint—ears attached to eyes that would roll, and a head that would bob in commiserating with her.

Small Talk

Though sensing this, I was still mildly surprised as she sidled up to me in the manner of a long-time confidant, for I had been led to expect more reserve in bridging the racial divide. Coming from a country where white people are mainly tourists and guests, I usually had no hang-ups in relating casually with them. It was the flaunted affluence and airs of some native, light-skinned highbrows, which drew lines that I had no desire to cross. However, I had received various well meant advisories that discouraged high expectations of interracial relations here. Furthermore, I had made one—only one—personal observation that reinforced the warning. So, I had recently been peering carefully over the horn-rims of inherited optimism.

This chatty senior was looking sideways at me now, soliciting agreement with her claim that the buses on this route were always too long in coming. I smiled a noncommittal response. How would I know—I who had only been there for the first time today, being less than three weeks in Canada, and still being caught unawares by vehicles driving on the right?

Still wondering why she had not moved away from the pedestrian crossing, I changed the subject slightly. Did she really think the buses would stop just there? She said they were supposed to, but I still had my doubts. I pictured a bus straddling the crossing, and it made no sense. Neither was the bus stop sign exactly at the crossing, though in my parochial experience it really seemed too close.

I turned the page on that thought as she began to rail against those bus drivers whom she said took delight in driving by. I couldn't imagine that either—having been struck by the politeness of the drivers I had travelled with since arriving in Canada. She should try getting a bus where I come from, I thought; but my voice chirped something like, "Never mind. I'm sure one will be here soon, and *he* will stop."

Oops—did I tell you I'm a novice at this political correctness thing? I find that trying to be correct for gender is threatening to stretch out my already too long sentences! Seriously though, I had never seen so many female bus drivers in my life! They made it seem like something I'd like to try. I mean, why not? If I, a graduate teacher of 19 years experience, was forced to consider packaging coins for pay in an OC Transpo vault, while the Ontario College of Teachers took months to scrutinise my credentials, why not cruise behind the wheel? I mean, theoretically a job is a job.

By then, I had shuffled far enough to the left that I was standing next to the bus stop pole, and the old lady had inched along after me. She was leaning toward me from time to time and looking downright conspiratorial. She even flashed her free hand at me at intervals to demand a more engaged response to her monologue, her fingers brushing me gently on the arm. A small group of school children had gathered on the other side of the pole, and they eyed us surreptitiously as we continued to exchange small talk.

Gut Feelings

Suddenly jumping to something more personal, my new acquaintance asked where I was from. When I told her, the name rang a bell, and she began to comment on what she'd heard about the climate. I prayed silently that she would not superimpose any negative stereotype on the visage before her.

Somehow, we got to the question of what I was doing on Bank Street, and I told her I was on the way home from the Catholic Immigration Centre, where I had gone for job-search assistance. At this, she launched into venting on the topic of immigrants who didn't really want to work, but just attached themselves to "these agencies" for benefits other than jobs. Then she waxed paramedical and started going on about Tuberculosis.

That's what her kind-hearted friend had got from volunteering at one of "those places"—from the immigrants of course! They were spreading T.B. to unsuspecting Canadians!

You could have struck me down with a feather—momentarily. I recovered quickly, concluding that the tube between her gut and her mouth was even shorter than mine, and certainly did not pass through the brain for censorship. She meant no harm—she was just a rattler—so I interjected innocently how surprised I was that such a thing could happen. How could it, when permanent residency applicants were so thoroughly screened for every malady under the sun? Oh, she quipped, it wasn't nice people like me who had come in legally that were the problem—it was the refugees with whom the government was being so lenient.

The smile never left my face—or my heart. I was truly amused. To reward my good-naturedness, she set about giving me her own job search advice. I looked like a nice, business-like lady; had I ever thought of working in an old folks' home? Where did I live anyway, and wasn't there one on the same road? Of course, I should try to get a job as a supervisor, not a caregiver. I did look like supervisor material.

Again, I made a noncommittal response that would have told my husband exactly what I was thinking. Then her eyes looked past me and I followed the gaze. Was that a bus coming at last? Yup, it was, so she wished me well, I reciprocated, and we both focused on the prospect of getting out of the chilly wind.

We had been there less than ten minutes—a fraction of the time I associated with waiting for a bus. I welcomed its spacious quietness, the blessing of being able to take a seat in safety, and the exchange of a cordial greeting with the driver. As I sat trying to memorise the brand new scenery and landmarks flashing by, the chuckle in my spirit oozed out to the corners of my mouth every so often, all along the 30 minute drive to the new address I was now calling home.

Chapter 10

Times and Seasons

Canada covers almost 7% of the earth's surface, an area of 9,970,610 square kilometers. However, its harsh climate has confined its development, and four-fifths of the country has never been permanently settled. Indeed, even perceptions of Canada have been distorted by its climate. The 18th century French philosopher, Voltaire, once described Canada as "a few acres of snow".[1]

October in Northeast Ontario. Nature displaying her broad pallet of hues. An inexpensive new camera clicking in the hands of its proud young owner, standing to practise her amateur art through the sun roof as Chief Cousin cruised. Along historic Colonel By Drive, the Rideau Canal lay cool and serene, forming a continuous backdrop for the trees which were the focus. Chief Cousin proudly pointed out his alma mater, Carleton University, nestled on its beautiful grounds in the "v" where the canal branched off from the Rideau River.

My Caribbean understanding of autumn colors, from pictures I had seen, proved but a pale shadow of reality. The Sunday before, Chief Cousin's sister, Jen, had taken us on an impromptu afternoon drive to Gatineau Park, which was the pride of local eco-tourism. We were actually returning home from church when she decided we should see "The Gatineau."

To get to the Gatineau Hills we drove farther into Quebec than we had previously been. So far, we had only visited Hull, where government offices spill over from downtown Ottawa across the river. I noticed the houses along

---

1.   Source: *Readers Digest Atlas of Canada*, 1995, p. 18

the route becoming more quaint as we neared Gatineau, some reminding me of pictures from the European story books I used to read as a child. Not quite the gingerbread house, but getting back there.

Jen's satisfaction, of course, was to hear us "ooh" and "aah" over the reds and oranges and purples and yellows and soft browns of arboreal beauty. The only disappointment was that we didn't have a camera that afternoon, for the treat had taken us by surprise. So, this later cruise along Colonel By was Chief Cousin's not-to-be-out-done gesture, to let us get the next best thing on film.

Thickening Blood?

Chameleon leaves were not all I noticed in this first autumn experience. As I expected, it was getting really chilly; but the physiological reactions I felt were unexpected. For one thing, I had more difficulty fasting than usual. And it was an inconvenient time for the body to crave more food, for I had decided to fortify my soul in this transition period with fasting.

Another change was that I very often had to fight drowsiness. This could have been induced by the self-inflicted low blood sugar, but I think it was more the temperature than anything. One morning, in a job-search workshop, the 10:30 break found me literally shaking my head to stay awake. Suddenly, I realized why "these people" drink so much coffee. Coffee is something for which I never developed a taste, either as a swotting student or as wife of a coffee grower. I had held a grudge against it ever since a doctor declared his suspicions about the role of caffeine addiction in my father's mid-life health problems.

So, I laughed at myself as I headed directly for the coffee cart at the break. Its bitter brew was suddenly an absolute necessity. Now I could make more sense of the clip-on coffee mugs without which some commuters seemed to feel undressed. I was more sympathetic toward the "high-schoolers" on the buses, whose balancing act with knapsacks, bus passes and brimming, disposable coffee cups threatened the cool, dry comfort of seated passengers.

They drank it not only for the warmth, I began to think, but also to avoid going into hibernation! Thank God, my body gradually adjusted as the temperatures sank toward their below-zero destination; for I really was not about to cultivate a taste for coffee. Someone asked me one day if my blood was now thickening, and it seemed a good explanation for why each cold spell left me less affected than the last.

With the falling temperatures of course, went sky-rocketing clothing bills. The price of business wear for winter conditions was really shocking. I found ways around it, for I'm not a slave to fashion; but it was vain to try coaxing my fashion-conscious teenagers to combine economy with protectiveness when selecting clothing. They didn't believe in layers, and their philosophy embraced single-purpose items that had to "look" better than they necessarily felt or functioned.

They preferred frozen ears and noses to a hood that fell a hair's breadth away from the current season's ill-defined norm. They preferred numb toes to the comfortable, inexpensive, warm but "ordinary" shoes that served my foot-mobiles. So, to avoid nursing the flu or constantly policing their attire, I just dug deep and forked out the cash.

Night and Day, Times Six

Night life has never interested me. My philosophy of both work and play has been, "Do it while it is day, for the night cometh when men should sleep. Selah." But as Ottawa's October gave way to November, the precious daylight time dwindled alarmingly, to a ridiculous eight hours. At 7:30 a.m. it was barely light, and by 3:30 p.m. it was dusk. At first, I got into a mad rush trying to complete all business by 3.30, before the darkness made the chill even colder.

Up to this point I also had a middle-class, Jamaican fear of being a pedestrian after dark; but soon, there was no getting away from it. There is just so much you can accomplish in eight hours. Besides, most business places would still be open for hours into the darkness. Buses would still be frequent, the streets and bus stops still relatively safe.

My early-to-bed sleep requirements were often satisfied long before dawn—a boon to creativity and devotions. So, the shift in daylight hours had a bright side. However, finding the bright side to people's assumption that one was available for business on Saturdays and Sundays was not so easy. Though not a Sabbath keeper, experience had taught me the role of a one-in-seven *rest* day, in maintaining *my* holistic wellness.

Nevertheless, even in this respect I had to adapt to the demands of this transition period. Eventually, I told myself, things would settle down and I would once more be able to call the shots. Job prospects being elusive, the idea of evening shift employment became palatable, though I still firmly rejected any hint of Sunday work. What I did resign myself to, however, was Sunday shopping. One had to eat, wear clothes and keep house, even with a schedule turned upside down.

Halloween

October 31, 1999, was our first experience of a Halloween-immersed society. It brought back two poignant memories of Octobers past. On that date 22 years earlier, I had given birth to our eldest daughter, largely oblivious to the furore that was being made elsewhere in the world over Halloween. It was not then celebrated in Jamaica. By 1979, however, I had not only become more aware of Halloween, but convinced of the incompatibility between these celebrations and devotion to Christ. This conviction cost me my job that school year.

We had a new principal who had recently returned from studies in the United States. She demanded total involvement from the staff in an elaborate Halloween observance at the school that October. I asked to be excused from active participation on religious grounds, explaining the violation of conscience I would otherwise suffer. As an alternative to taking the day off, I offered to provide classroom supervision for children when they were not in the planned pageant; but the idea was rejected.

This was a prestigious private school, affiliated to a mainline denominational church; and the principal took deep offence at what she interpreted as an indictment against her own religious outlook. I appealed to the minister of the church, and he tried to represent my viewpoint to her with more expert diplomacy—all to no avail. The lady was totally unwilling to excuse me, so I absented myself on October 31 without her sanction. Our relationship never recovered, and after serving my students well for the remainder of the school year, I resigned the position.

So here we were, our first October in Canada, surrounded with ghoulish decorations as far as the eye could see. Pumpkins were no longer just an ingredient for my favorite soups, and ghost-considerations were no longer relegated to serious discussions about spirits. We were practically tripping over witches on broomsticks in the mall and school hallways, and I was walking past ghouls posted on hedges all along the avenue. It was as if these characters had all escaped from the books that had been banned in our household.

The whole affair took on an air of legitimacy, complete with a vocabulary that was new to us. Wicca? Wiccan? As temporary single parent, I mandated that Deb and Joe keep out of the celebrations at school, and suffered through having to pretend that no-one was home when the neighborhood kids came trick-or-treating in the night. We had to pretend, because we were still guests in someone else's house, and that's how they handled it. My choice would have been to explain to callers that life was proceeding normally for us, and we didn't celebrate Halloween. Given half a chance, I would also have told them why.

A Good Report

One evening in early November, I marched briskly along the 10-minute route to the high school, for some face to face with Joe's teachers. Despite the clothing zipped up to my chin, I kept a brisk pace—not because it was late, but for the maximum warmth that my legs could generate. The hood pulled close around my face had almost the effect of blinders. Nevertheless, a bright, new glimmer caught my eye. It came from little red lights strung out over the evergreens, where orange Halloween decorations had recently hung. I could hardly believe it; but obviously, these were heralds of Christmas, still almost seven weeks away.

It was the first evening scheduled for Grade 11 parent-teacher interviews, and the report cards had been sent home a few days earlier. Both Deb and Joe had received pleasing reports, and I went to the Grade 12 evening a few nights later. I needed not only to meet the teachers, but to quiz them about the things a report card can't convey. "Pleasing" was not our goal. "Excellent" was where we had to aim.

Most importantly, at this early stage of the game, I wanted the teachers' impressions on how Deb and Joe were relating to them and their classmates. Was there a comfortable rapport developing? Were they doing what the teachers expected of them, and if not, how could I help? Also, were there any recommendations about course selections for the coming semester, or were the initial selections still making sense?

The teachers' responses relieved me almost completely. They were happy with my teenagers, who (I had already gathered at home) were equally happy with them. The things I could help with at home were defined for me, and I had their word on what was needed in the pursuit of excellent averages. All accomplished in a totally pleasant atmosphere. This was good!

The tales already brought home from school had been an education in themselves. Some things were totally shocking to me—like the regulation permitting students to smoke on the compound at designated times and places. Some were just extremes of what I had half expected to hear. For example, the foul language that students commonly used was a tack-on to the insolence I had heard is often meted out to teachers in First World classrooms.

But others were just an education. It was through the school that Ottawa's multiculturalism was really fleshed out for us. On a single compound, the kids were rubbing shoulders with people from all over the world, as well as native Canadians. Their personal acquaintance had suddenly been broadened to include: other Caribbean and Latin American nationals, Americans, Asians, British, Egyptians, Ethiopians, Indians, Iranians, Irish, Italians, Kuwaitis, Lebanese, Nigerians, Palestinians, Romanians, Somalis, Turks, Yugoslavians, and of course, others from every continent.

I Am Jamaican

More people from the hot spots of the world, than from peaceful countries, seem to have landed in Canada. Having arrived in significant numbers, some were keeping their own cultures largely intact, while others were better able to integrate. We discovered (as I'm sure the RCMP[2] also has) that some youngsters who came from war-torn countries had volatile tempers and unreasoning loyalties. We realized that here, Jamaicans were not always regarded as the most aggressive people, as we had heard that some thought us to be.

The most surprising thing was the attitude of other students to Jamaicans. It was both flattering and alarming, drawing various responses from the Jamaican students at the school. On one hand, their peers were fascinated by our accent, and regarded the Jamaican Creole with more respect than some of us did at home. They couldn't understand it; so, in their multilingual setting, it was yet another language that they wanted to learn. To us it had always been just "patois"—the common man's potent blend of English, Spanish and African languages, brewed over time, and spiked with mystique because of the grass roots' need to be obscure to the ears of the "busha"[3].

---

2. Royal Canadian Mounted Police
3. Originally, "slave-master, plantation owner." Later, just a term applied to the privileged class.

Some Jamaican students exploited this to the maximum, embellishing their Creole with deep rural accents, the better to exclude others from their conversation. An amusing incident took place on a bus one afternoon, as a result of this. Two Jamaican girls came on, and proceeded to "labrish"[4] about various people in the bus, in what Kingstonians might call a deep, St. Elizabeth patois. Complete strangers, they soon began to eye Joseph. First they agreed that he was probably Somali, as he did not look Jamaican at all. Then they gaily began to comment on his good looks and lament the fact that he wasn't Jamaican. When he couldn't take it any more without laughing, he turned to them and identified himself. That put an end to the labrish.

On the other hand, the youth culture here was enamoured with an image of Jamaica that revolved around beaches, reggae music, Bob Marley's legacy, dreadlocks, and marijuana ("ganja"). They didn't believe it when Deb and Joe said they had never smoked ganja and didn't revere Bob Marley. But they were still happy to exchange language lessons—a little Jamaican patois for a little Somali, French or Arabic.

With respect to the language and demeanor of the popular youth culture, Deb and Joe would just have to swim harder against the tide than they were accustomed to doing, with as much grace as they could muster. As the weeks wore on, they became more experienced than ever in the practical application of Paul's words: "As far as it depends on you, live at peace with everyone."[5] As for me, I just decided to maintain vigilance against their adopting any undesirable, new behaviours at home, or—as far as I was able—at school.[6]

---

4. Jamaican Creole for "chatter, gossip", used as a noun or verb.
5. Romans 12:18
6. For more reactions to the falling temperatures, see Appendix (letter to Assistant Teachers at the mission school, dated October 20, 1999; and letter to Household/Farm Employee, dated October 24, 1999)

Chapter 11

Water, Water Everywhere

"Whosoever will, let him take the water of life freely."
Revelation 22:17, the Bible, King James Version.

The schedule of activities in my hand was catchy and promising. It was part of the visitor's packet I had received at the second Ottawa church I visited, only that morning. The church was just next-door, which could allow full involvement and discourage Sunday morning bench-warming. This would help to keep us on the cutting edge of a dynamic Christianity, as we had been before coming to Canada.

This church's main youth meeting was on Fridays, the same school-facilitating night as the one our teens used to attend at great inconvenience in Kingston, so far from the district where we lived. Here, they also had the option of getting involved in an indoor sporting activity at the church on Saturdays. I didn't see any outlets for drama, band, or junior worship-leading advertised on the brochure, but you (sometimes) can't have it all.

My choices included a couple of prayer meetings, a fortnightly house fellowship not far away, and a weekly interest group whose label attracted me as something I had pursued at home. The latter was also held just across the street, and I decided to sample it the following week, rather than try to arrange night-time transportation to attend a house fellowship.

Church # 3

So, it was just curiosity and an already accepted invitation from Cousin Jen, that led me to yet another church that evening. She was a member of that church. She thought the service was to begin at 6 p.m., and that we were late as we sped across town, and hurried across the parking lot toward the building. I had just enough time to notice that its architecture was slightly more imaginative than the cuboid design of the church building next-door. However, once inside, I compared the scene with mental sketches of the other modern, North American church buildings I had visited, and noticed a trend. All the "sanctuaries" were of the same basic shape: semicircular around a relatively large stage, with the floor sloping gently toward the front.

Many interiors in Jamaica still shared a similar floor plan to that of the old traditional church we visited the week before; the pulpit and choir stall smaller and facing a more or less rectangular area of closely packed pews. However, some of our newer Christian groups used halls and rented facilities not designed for the purpose, where they freely arranged furniture for their immediate need, and sometimes had no suitable stage. This lent fluidity to the proceedings, facilitating the focus on individuals rather than pews. It also put the leadership in the position of having to rely more on dynamism than on physical elevation, to hold and direct the attention of the congregation.

Here at Church # 3, I saw an encouraging amount of floor space around the altar, and aisles widening toward the back of the sanctuary. About two-thirds of the way back, they intersected a broad aisle that formed an arc across the sanctuary, completing the circles of opportunity for freedom of movement. It brought to mind one of the small Pentecostal congregations in the mountain districts where we had laboured. They had a choir that often became a jogging band, encircling the congregation to an inimitable beat while they sang. As I remembered the overflowing attendance I had witnessed there, and the bare facilities they had managed to erect, I reflected that they would truly have relished all this carpeted space.

Contrary to our fears, we weren't late for the service. There was a business meeting in progress, which had been scheduled to put the regular worship service back by an hour. At home, this would have been a members-only meeting; so at first I felt a bit out of place. However, no-one seemed distracted, and we sat close to the back, where I was able to relax and pay careful attention to the proceedings.

"Occupy Till I Come"

The leadership of this church seemed to include very astute managers, if their financial report was taken at face value. Their human efforts also seemed to have been met with divine blessing; for some church coffers, from what I understood, did not similarly reflect the financial expertise that I was sure many church boards could boast.

Among other things, the report dealt with the pros and cons of strategies to maximise profits from their real estate holdings. I could hear the leadership wrestling with their choices: should they continue servicing high overheads to facilitate out-of-town ministries, or rather, dispose of a particular expensive facility? It threw up the challenge of how to apply Jesus' teachings on stewardship and investment, so that they would not contravene the principles of charity and faith. One thing was certainly obvious: these folks were not queuing up for Jesus' rebuke to "unprofitable, lazy servants," spoken in the Parable of the Long Journey.[1] They were acting on His mandate, "Occupy till I come."

When the worship service began, I was thrilled to bits by the jubilance of the congregation. Here, my own "hind's feet"[2] would be lost in a crowd and not create a spectacle. The beat was different from my favorite variety, but the songs were just as inspired, prophetic and triumphant. One I had never heard before, which I dubbed "Behold He comes," struck a particular chord in my spirit, released the springs in my legs, and would remain with me for days. I later discovered, as I searched the Christian bookstore for a tape, that its title was really, "Days of Elijah."

Words In Season

There was a visiting preacher as guest speaker that evening. Both his introduction by the senior pastor, and his own sharing, took me one step further along a certain obstacle course on which God had started me some time before. It concerned the relationship between the Church and the Jews. I took notes avidly. There was even a bonus thrown in, which offered a plausible and appealing rationale for why so many Christian immigrants had found themselves in Canada, some against their best intentions. Wow! Words in

---

1.   Luke 19: 11-26. See also Matthew 25: 14-29.

2.   2 Samuel 22:34, Psalm 18:33, Habakkuk 3:19, King James Version

season… Was this particular "word" and its premise of a special, divine plan for Canada a true "rhema,"[3] or was it just flattering? I'd have to research that some more.

Something else I'd have to research was the strange noises that could be heard coming from the seating area at the back of the sanctuary. I had noticed that some severely disabled people were seated in their wheelchairs in that section, and some were being quite vocal in their own way. But the sounds were definitely not coming from them alone. Without turning to stare, I could also detect unusual movements and postures being adopted by at least one person who had not seemed mentally impaired.

I remembered the news of the "Toronto Blessing," which had reached us in Jamaica some time before. Some members of our church had wanted to visit Toronto for a first-hand impression of what was happening, but the cost was prohibitive. Amidst the reports of familiar but rare divine unction, we had heard of unfamiliar "manifestations," which included people making animal noises and strange movements, ostensibly in response to some act of the Holy Spirit.

Now I wondered if this was what I was glimpsing here. From the business meeting, the worship, and the preaching, I went home lifted; but from these other aspects of the service I was also bemused.

Back to Church # 2

By mid-week, there was a very encouraging "welcome" letter in our mailbox from the senior pastor of Church # 2, in response to the visitor's questionnaire I had completed on Sunday morning. At the appointed time of my chosen, special-interest meeting, I ventured once more across the street; but this time met with a disappointing anticlimax. I had misinterpreted the title of the meeting to suggest something of an outreach activity, whereas the focus was inward and the approach rather passive. "Oh, well," I thought, "I've been there and done that before; there's no reason to retrace those steps. Perhaps the prayer meeting would be more mutually beneficial."

So, the next Sunday morning, at the time of the pre-service prayer meeting, I asked directions to the prayer room and entered expectantly. Once through the door, I almost instinctively tip-toed to the nearest seat. There

---

3.   Greek: utterance (of God) specific to a person or situation, rather than generally applicable as the words of scripture ("logos")

were a few people inside, all quiet and immobile, not interacting at all with each other, but presumably with God. "I can do this," I thought as I knelt very carefully for fear of causing the least disturbance. "But I could also have done it by myself at home. What's the point of the people?"

The fact that I was the only black person in the room wasn't my problem, and I dutifully began praying for all the strangers around me. Soon, I heard a welcome sound—a human voice calling us together to close the session corporately. Promising—but again an anti-climax, for any group participation in this last prayer was silent.

As most people dispersed quietly afterwards, I overheard something that identified the last pray-*er* as the senior pastor. Determined to redeem the time, I went and introduced myself to him. He, in turn, introduced me to others who had lingered around him; but they were all a bit reserved, and I neither heard nor felt anything of the warmth his letter had seemed to extend.

In the sanctuary, I found my kids, who had arrived just in time for the service. It was their first visit here, and I was eager to have them test the waters. Without Christian fellowship at school, their nurture had to take priority over all else in our choice of a new church home. We had all been encouraged by the previous week's announcement that over 30 youth were away from church at a camp. In our experience, youth group vitality indicated life in a church, because hum-drum routine doesn't cut it with youth.

In the middle of the service when the call went out, the kids went off with the other youth to "class." I hoped they would find fellowship that was comfortable, while continuing to "provoke" them to righteousness in the spirit of Hebrews 10:24.[4]

I enjoyed the service as I had the first time, for the Holy Spirit was manifestly present; but afterwards, a chill wind met me in the lobby, when I went to the counter to ask about a certain brochure. The gentleman whom I tried to ask kept looking pointedly away—for so long that I figured there was something wrong. Wasn't I speaking loudly enough, or was my accent that thick? I turned to a lady and got my question partially answered.

As God would have it, she handed me over for the completion to the same man I had been trying to address, and now he had no choice but to speak with me. Poor thing, he did manage a smile and I smiled back.

---

4.   "And let us consider one another, to provoke unto love and to good works." (King James Version)

By this time, the kids were ready and we set off on our brief walk. A wind had given teeth to the midday chill, so it was not till we were safely indoors again that we could compare notes. They were no more excited about the Senior High class than I was about the prayer meeting or the cool reception at the welcome counter; but I still hoped that weekend youth group involvement would make a difference. Could it be that this convenient next-door church was really not the one after all?

Timing and Purpose

We passed on the offer of their evening service, in order to revisit Church # 3. The week before, the kids had stood among immigrants and other youth called forward for special prayer, and I had gleaned prophetic significance from one intercessor's utterances. As she laid hands on them and prayed, her words and facial expression had briefly dipped into a valley of "difficulties" and come quickly through to a brighter place—the place of fulfilment of specific purposes—in God, *and in Canada.*

I knew the kids didn't relish being put on the spot in this new environment, but interactive ministry was what they were accustomed to, and they had enjoyed the exuberance of the worship as well as the spontaneity that the Holy Spirit was "allowed."

The following Sunday, we returned there to sample the morning service, which Cousin Jen said was a more formal occasion. She said that pants were not thought the best attire for ladies at this service, which was a pity; for just four weeks into the transition from a tropical to an Ottawa autumn, I had concluded that my legs would only be comfortable in pants.

Braving the chill so as not to offend, I dutifully wore the longest skirt I could find, with a suitable assortment of undergarments. I was not enjoying the new wardrobe demands imposed by the climate, but the promise of satisfying my Berean[5] curiosity was worth the risk of discomfort. Mona Fellowship, where we had grown for the past 18 years, was noted for training members to "prove all things"[6] by measuring doctrine and practice against the plumb line of scripture; and it had become second nature.

So, I was setting out to see if all that glittered here was gold. From my observation of televangelists' ministries, many North Americans seemed gullible

---

5.   Acts 17:11b
6.   1 Thessalonians 5:21

in spiritual matters, given to some excess, hysteria and "band-wagoning". Since excitement is not an end in itself for me, I needed to experience enough of what obtained in the *life* of this very appealing church, to judge the carats of the glitter.

Food for Thought

As we had been told, the Sunday morning service was more quiet and formal than the evening; but I needn't have bothered to wear a skirt. There were enough women comfortably dressed in slacks, to make it a non-issue. And it wasn't that everyone had stiffened, for some worshippers still exercised the freedom to take their energetic praise right down to the wide space around the platform. Footloose and quite uninhibited, yet totally "decent and in order,"[7] they enjoyed the apparent approval of the leadership just as much as those who remained in their pews. Nor was there any attempt from the pulpit to *demand* more exuberance from the quieter worshipers. The worship leaders *led*, they didn't *goad*.

When the Senior Pastor took the lead, two of his actions surprised me. Both involved declarations of faith which he asked the congregation to repeat after him. That, in itself, was not unusual. What struck me was that they were apparently well known and *regular repetitions*—something I hadn't come across in renewed churches, where recitations I learnt in childhood such as the Apostle's Creed, the Lord's Prayer and the 23rd Psalm seemed to have lost their appeal.

I listened carefully. One of the confessions affirmed belief in the Bible, laid claim to all its promises, and identified one's self fully with its profile of the believer. The other prepared the congregation for the offering, declaring them to be "tithers" and laying claim to the associated blessings promised in Malachi 3:10–11. Reflecting on this well known passage, I found the pastor's extrapolations to modern economic life astounding enough to commission a thoughtful re-examination.

When I asked Jen why so much information was requested on the outside of the offering envelopes, she said it allowed givers to be issued tax credit receipts at year end, as offerings were tax deductible. At that, my mind went into Jamaican Creole, "But si ya mi Lawd... Wat a ting!"[8] Nothing to scoff at, mind you. At first thought, it seemed to detract from the sacrificial aspect of giving; but perhaps it contributed to the prosperity of the church, which they had been sharing, as I had heard before.

---

7.   1 Corinthians 14:40
8.   "Look, Lord! What a strange thing!"

Nothing else disturbed my antennae that morning, and if I were one of those suspect reporters who used to rate church services in Jamaica for the media, I would have given it a top rating. But mine is not the opinion that counts, is it? From comparisons with Biblical examples, I think God was well pleased with the heart these people displayed toward Him. At least they were in no peril from the school-marmish letter of the law, which kills through it's preoccupation with dotting of i's and crossing of t's.

A Warmer Welcome

Their visitors' welcome routine was pleasantly personal. Welcome cards were slipped to you by some nearby person on your pew, rather than by an usher. At the end of the service you were invited to the Visitors' Centre, really a comfortable lounge where literature, coffee, and other refreshments could be had while you interacted with members on duty there, and whoever else wondered in. The pastor with responsibility for Cell Ministry, and his wife, were the ones who met with visitors that morning. They made certain that we had brochures and schedules of the church's activities, and that the church had our contact information.

While we chatted, a very friendly member with teenagers of her own came into the room, searching for someone, and conveniently abandoned her search to join the welcome activities. Convenient for us, as she proved to be really interested in getting to know us, and having the two sets of teens get together. When she discovered that we had no car and would probably have difficulty attending regularly, she not only offered to transport us on Sunday mornings, but started investigating whom she could draft into including the kids in a Wednesday night car pool, for the youth meeting.

I was truly impressed with this lady, and with the whole atmosphere. Then, the youth pastor also passed through the room, and that was a shocker. He looked barely older than a teen himself. He had neither abandoned the garb nor the lingo, and they were not tack-ons either. He was the genu-I-ne article; from the flopping of the pants around his ankles to the crown of his hairstyle. And our brief exchange, of which the kids understood more than I did, left the impression that he was as zealous a Christian as they come. I smiled, Deb flashed her infectious, 16-year-old grin, and Joe gave a cool, 15-year-old nod of approval.

Chapter 12

A Cold Sweat

2001 census figures show Ontario unemployment for the over-15 population at only 6.3%[1], which is low by Third World standards; but what percent of those unemployed or under-employed are immigrants?

Having passed the SI Number barrier in early October meant that my documentation to apply for registration to teach in Ontario was complete. On the way to send the forms off in the mail, I stopped in at one of the immigrant assistance agencies. There, I was invited to leave my submission with them, as there was a batch for several immigrant teachers being sent to the OCT (Ontario College of Teachers) under their auspices the very next day. The counselor thought it should expedite the processing of the applications if they went in together.

I hesitated for more than a moment, strangely disquieted at the prospect of leaving my large envelope of tediously gathered documents there, rather than just putting a stamp on it and committing it to Canada Post as I had planned. Our talk had revealed that the gentleman was new to his job. In fact, he seemed to know less about the OCT submission requirements than I did. The bulky envelope in my hand represented the completion of a process Mike had insisted that I begin long before leaving Jamaica. But then, this counselor represented officialdom, which could perhaps indeed lend some weight to my application.

---

1. Statistics Canada's Internet Site, http://www.statcan.ca/english/Pgdb/People/Labour/labour07b.htm, August 12, 2002

We talked on, and wisdom failed me when I let his pitch drown out the still, small voice of caution. Not wanting to appear distrusting, I handed it over and went on my way. The busyness of life took over while I waited to hear from the OCT, and a few weeks passed. I had been advised to allow three months for processing, but late in October, something prompted me to call Toronto for an update on the status of my application. The voice at the other end said it had not been received.

As a true Jamaican storyteller would say, "Col' sweat wash mi!"[2] I called the gentleman who had taken my submission, and was not very calm in communicating my distress, disappointment and alarm. When he seemed to have no explanation for the situation, I didn't mince words or hide my annoyance. He said that as far as he knew, the batch of applications had been dispatched, but his co-worker who had the details to answer my questions was not in office that day. He would take it up with her tomorrow; they would pursue the matter and get back to me. I should give him two days.

Perhaps I had formed too elevated an opinion of Canadian bureaucracy too soon, stupidly forgetting about the human fallibility that one should expect. Nevertheless, this situation seemed downright uncanny. As always, when a new boulder that seemed bigger than the average appeared in our path, I invested in a long distance call to Mike in Jamaica. After posing all the questions for which I had no answers, he understood the situation and we prayed.

Two days and various apologies later, the OCT assured me of the documents being in their possession. The strange tale was that they had been sent to the wrong department, and not re-routed till my call alerted someone to the mistake. My question at this point, for which I could get no direct answer, was, "Having in effect lost a month, will I have to wait *another* three months for this process to be over?"

A Place of our Own

In 1996, 63,315 of Ottawa's 385,140 households lived in apartments, five or more storeys high, and 1,570 households lived in "movable dwellings"[3] (mobile homes?)

---

2.   Jamaican Creole meaning, "I was so frightened that I broke into a cold sweat."

3.   Statistics Canada's Internet Site, http://statcan.ca/english/Pgdb/People/ Families/families55e.htm, August 13, 2002

By late October, we knew we needed to find a place of our own. Mike would be back for a while at Christmas, with Arianne on her first visit. Chief Cousin's sons would also be home for Christmas, with friends, needing the space we were occupying. In anticipation, we had bought bits of furniture and equipment at bargain prices here and there, and they were stacked in Chief Cousin's garage.

Even before Mike left, we had made a tentative arrangement by phone to rent a three bedroom apartment which would become vacant in December. When I went to make the deposit, however, new conditions came into play. The agent said that because we still had no steady Canadian income, we would have to pay six months' rent in advance. Chief Cousin offered to stand surety for us, but this would not suffice. Besides, once I saw the size of the rooms, it took no more time to decide that this was not the place. Everything would be just too cramped.

So, I scanned the papers daily for rental accommodation as well as employment opportunities. In some respects, Mike is more a dreamer than I am, and every now and then he entertained the "option" of purchasing rather than renting. We hadn't paid rent in 20 years, and I suppose he just didn't see himself as a tenant. Chief Cousin, who did not share my aversion to wild goose chases, encouraged him.

I steered them away from this train of thought as much as possible. How could we consider buying when we hadn't even settled the employment questions? What if we had to move to Toronto where the job market was reportedly better? Furthermore, wouldn't a down-payment just now be impossible, as we had decided not to sell our house in Jamaica? We had been mortgage-free for over 12 years, and somehow, the prospect of a new mortgage scared me more than that of tenancy. Furthermore, in Jamaica, buying a house is something that ties you up in legal and stress knots for months.

This particular Saturday, however, I wasn't thinking of the issue at all— just relaxing with the papers and having a good read. The ad literally jumped out at me as I turned a page. A newly refurbished set of townhouses, one phase in the renovation of an entire community, was on the market with features and financing options that excited even me. The deposit was 5%, the projected mortgage payments compared favorably with the rent we were prepared to pay, and the deal included a new fridge, stove and dishwasher. Chief Cousin and I went there that very evening.

The model units could hardly have looked better. They were very spacious, excellently refurbished, and the developers offered a range of choices for customizing the finish. The catch was that we had discovered the scheme late, and the special financing offer was only available for a few more days. That night I was on the phone to Mike, and having heard as much as he could at Bell Canada's rates, he agreed that he would allow himself 24 hours to pray about it, and call us back the following evening after church.

Sunday evening brought his go-ahead, and on October 24, I made the initial (refundable) deposit on the only remaining unit of the particular design that seemed most suitable. By now, I had Mike's job letter from the Ottawa branch of his company, and the salesperson did not forewarn us that we might have difficulty qualifying for the mortgage. On October 28 I signed the initial sale agreement.

The following two weeks were spent faxing correspondence back and forth from Jamaica. By the first weekend, we had been disqualified for the special financing offer of the bank involved, because most of our assets were still off-shore. So, the following week we tried a mortgage broker, who eventually found us the necessary financing, once we agreed to double the deposit to 10%. On November 11th I signed an amendment to the sale agreement and we made a second deposit on the 18th, with a closing date of December 17, 1999.

Some documents had to be sent by FedEx rather than fax. Then, there were the inter-bank transfers that cost so much in fees at the Jamaican end. But by mid-November everything was in place. We looked forward confidently to making the final deposit, and taking possession on the promised date in December. Given our Jamaican experience of buying houses, I could hardly believe that the business had been transacted in such a short time, and so relatively simply.

We had gained invaluable experience and made important contacts in the few weeks' process. I was now on good terms with a lawyer and a mortgage broker. Mike and I had gotten Power of Attorney documents drawn up, which, in our situation, we should have thought of earlier. We had learnt about CMHC[4] mortgage insurance that is legally required with a deposit less than 25%. It took a while for me to understand this, as we had no equivalent in Jamaica, and I kept confusing it with house insurance.

Then, I set about purchasing the basic furniture and appliances that we still needed. Again, the identity and credit issues came up, beginning with "no Canadian driver's license;" so Chief Cousin helped by letting me make the purchases in his name where necessary. Only the largest items were to be

---

4.   Canada Mortgage and Housing Corporation

delivered to the house after we took possession. Everything else we stockpiled in Chief Cousin's garage. Finally, we arranged to rent a large van, with his son as driver, to make the move.

"Dutty Tough"

By mid-December, we felt it was really cold. All the locals said it was "mild," and laughed at our shivering as they spun tales of harsh winters past. They shuddered themselves, to tell about the 1998 ice storm, a winter catastrophe that had nonetheless produced very photogenic scenery—if you like sparkling, translucent white. Listening to predictions of how cold it could become, I remembered hearing a radio talk-show in Jamaica, in which a returning emigrant said she had come back to avoid being buried in England, for the ground there was just too cold. She should have tried the ground in Ottawa, where householders are warned, as winter approaches, to lock off water to outside taps so that the ice won't burst them.

The first flurries of snow had surprised us one day on the way home from church. They were just tiny, white specks blowing about in the air, and melting as soon as they hit the windshield. The first real snowfall came at night. I was awakened earlier than usual in the morning by a strange glow coming through the bedroom window. When I got up and looked out, there was a blanket of white over the street and pavements, white capping on the roofs that I could see, and blobs of white decorating trees and shrubs. It gave an unfamiliar reflection of what light there was, creating the glow that had awakened me before 5 a.m.

We discovered that some people here hardly think it's cold till the temperature falls beyond minus 20 degrees. Thank God it's Celsius. By that time, believe me, "dutty tough!"[5] We soon found that it can also be very slippery. On December 18 when we were to move house, only the exertion numbed the bite of the chill.

It was a fair Saturday morning, and we had the unexpected task of collecting some bedroom furniture from a warehouse, as the store was having problems with their deliveries, and wanted to reschedule ours. We couldn't accommodate the proposed new schedule, so we opted to collect it ourselves. That became trip number 1, as the boxes would fill the whole van, if they fit at all.

---

5.   Jamaican Creole meaning, "the ground (or life) is hard (impenetrable to the farmer's tools.)" This reflection is also the theme of Louise Bennett's poem, "Dutty Tough," in her beloved anthology, *Jamaica Labrish*.

At the warehouse, the boxes were larger than we expected. But we packed and packed: Joe, the delivery clerk and I. In the cab of the van, the radio was tuned to Carleton University's CKCU FM. Their Saturday afternoon program, Reggae in the Fields, was on for some time before we realized that their special guest was Cousin Jen. Between proudly listening to her Jamaican accent, and warming to the boldness with which she brought her best friend, God, into this secular, Rastafarian-flavored program, we continued to wedge the boxes into every inch of space.

Finally, everything was in, with just enough space left up front for Joe's frame. Now that we knew the size and weight of the boxes, we realized there was no way they were going to get from the parking lot and up the little hill to our new home, with the limited manpower we had. So, the next stop was Canadian Tire, to find an affordable hand truck. Minutes later, we returned to the van with one, and slid it into the narrow space between the boxes and the back doors, which—miraculously—seemed reserved for its specific dimensions.

The move took a couple more trips across town, and a lot of energy (without much sweat, as it was too cold). Only for the last trip did Deb happily prepare to climb into the van. She had spent the day dutifully cleaning up after us, carefully returning our cousins' house to guest-ready condition.

As we inched toward the front door, Chief Cousin looked wistful. He had enjoyed the kids' presence: Deb's effervescence, Joe's "man-to"[6] company and the Jamaicanisms which reminded him of home. I had been particularly blessed by Chief Cousin's tales of my father's kindness to him and his siblings, which he modestly said he had only repaid in his hospitality to us. Daddy had been their favorite Uncle, taking them for long, exciting rides when motoring was still a novelty to the rural Jamaican family; and doing other activities with them when his older brother, their Dad, was too busy. I had also enjoyed getting to know Claire, and hearing her take on events that I had been too young to remember.

But eventually, we left, and drove across town for the last time that day. When the door finally closed us into our own home, there was deep relief. The tiredness we felt was the happy, satisfied kind, though there was still much to do. Of necessity, it was also the kind where hyper-stimulation takes over for a while, so the adrenaline kept pumping till we had at least the beds out of boxes and assembled. I think you know what happened then.[7]

---

6.   Jamaican Creole description of precocious manhood

7.   For other events surrounding the move, see Appendix (letter to Home Church Brethren in Jamaica and the US, of January 8, 2000, 6:23 a.m.)

Chapter 13

Millennium

As a child, I looked forward to the year 2000, when, if I survived, I would become 46 years old. Surviving would be a great achievement, for I was a very sickly child.

11 p.m., December 31, 1999. We were seated all in a row, in church: Mike to my right with Joseph next to him, Deborah to my left, and next to her, "big sister" Arianne (who was actually the most petite of our girls.) I felt comforted that at least five of our seven were here together for the impending, momentous occasion. Despite the debate fueled by the press on whether it was 2000 or 2001 that should bear the honor, we sided with popular public opinion, which had declared 12:01 a.m., just minutes away, the dawn of a new millennium.

Gail and Sean were in Jamaica—she visiting from college with Grandma and friends; he mostly with his fiancée's family. It was the first Christmas holiday that we hadn't been all together, and only the second we had ever spent away from Jamaica. Mike and Ari had been here with us for nine days, and they would be gone again in three.

Arianne's application for a visitor's visa had first been denied by the Canadian High Commission in Jamaica. That was a shock. She had applied for a multiple-entry visa, which seemed the logical thing if half of her family now lived in Canada. We had no idea permission to visit would have been denied. Tearfully disappointed, she had appealed the decision with Mike's help, and been granted a single-entry visa. The application fee for that was half of what she had paid; but, in continuing defiance of logic, there was no refund.

All that forgotten like labor pains, they had come bringing Jamaican Christmas cakes, rum-spiked Sorrel drink, other treats from our loved ones, and discreet whispers of what gifts they had to leave behind because there was just too much luggage. They were pleased as punch with the new house, for they hadn't known exactly what to expect. In just a couple of days, Mike had met the neighbors, installed the blinds and curtain rods, and taken over the settling-in arrangements that I was only too glad to relinquish for a while.

Ari had never been in winter conditions before, so she eagerly took it all in before the novelty froze. Joe outdid himself trying to get her excited about his favorite haunts: the almost frozen-over creek and the now skeletal "green space" west of us. But Deb's introduction to the bargain stores in nearby shopping malls was more to Ari's liking.

At first, we took them around by bus, showing off our mastery of the public transportation system and the geography; but being stranded at a bus station on Christmas Eve after a late movie had put an end to that. We soon rented a car for respite from the cold, and to use our sight-seeing time more efficiently. In Jamaica, Christmas decorations are not nearly as elaborate as those here, where the displays on both public buildings and homes seem to compete with each other. So, there was a lot to see; and, suddenly the proud tour guide, I navigated.

Now, introducing them to the church I hoped we'd continue to call home, I was a bit nervous—just too eager for them to be impressed. In religious practice, I was the most radical member of the family. The others were more moderate, and I was afraid they would find this atmosphere, which so delighted me, a bit extreme. Deb and Joe had not been much help in campaigning, for trying to fit in with new peers still challenged their comfort zones. But they did concede that we hadn't found a more promising congregation to date.[1]

Common sense had dictated that we try the affiliated assembly just a few bus stops away from our new house, for the church we had been attending was now even farther away than before we moved. On Christmas Sunday, we had taken a taxi for the short ride to the nearer assembly, because it was snowing heavily, and the bus schedule is slowed on Sundays. The members and leaders we met were good hosts, but the "full-and-bubbling-over" kind of spiritual exuberance was missing. Deb and Joe had testified with me to this

---

1.   For more church observations to date, see Appendix (letter to Best Friend C, dated November 12, 1999).

fact, between chattering teeth, as we waited afterwards in the bus shelter for what seemed a very long time.

So, here we were now, at Church # 3, sitting close to the back where Mike was most comfortable, and observing as much as participating in the proceedings. The program planned for this auspicious night was suitably unique, and I thought, just what the Doctor had ordered—at least for Arianne. Drama was her thing. As a keen member of the drama company affiliated to our Jamaican home church, her debut had not only brought flattering response, but confirmed to her the possibilities for this vehicle of ministry.

After the opening praise and worship, the program that unfolded as the clock ticked toward midnight was pure pageantry, which climaxed in a wedding to which the whole congregation had been invited. We were told the couple had wanted to be married at the precise turn of the century, and it made the day (or night) for many present. The novelty of the proceedings, the festive, bubbling excitement in the air, and the scrutiny of "John and Jenny Public" only seemed to enhance the solemnization of their vows.

The Right New Beginnings?

My best present was late for Christmas, but I got it in time for the New Year jubilation. It was a letter from the OCT[2], dated December 23, 1999, which read:

> *"In consideration of your academic and professional education, you are hereby issued this Letter of Eligibility, valid for three years under Section 14(1) of Regulation 184/97 made under the Ontario College of Teachers Act, 1996. When you have conformed with the requirements of Section 15 of Regulation 184/97, you will qualify for an Interim Certificate of Qualification valid in: Primary and Junior Divisions..."*

The accompanying literature explained that this only allowed one to seek employment as a teacher in Ontario, and it was not a teaching certificate. To

---

2.   Ontario College of Teachers

convert this Letter of Eligibility to an Interim Certificate of Qualification, one had to:

> "...obtain an acceptable offer of employment as a teacher from: a school board, a private school, the Provincial Schools Authority in Ontario, the Department of Indian Affairs and Northern Development of the Government of Canada, or a council of a band or a Native education authority that provides education for Native People."

The offer of employment could be for a contract position or for "supply" (substitute) teaching, and must be confirmed on the original Letter of Eligibility by the signature of an approved Supervisory Officer. The second half-page of instructions defined the appropriate "Supervisory Officer," and the procedure in each of the various circumstances under which one could be hired. It concluded with, "You must apply for membership in the College by submitting your original Letter of Eligibility (appropriately signed) and the $90 annual membership fee."

The Interim Certificate of Qualification could, in turn, be converted into a Certificate of Qualification after one had completed 200 days of "successful, appropriate Ontario teaching experience." Only this latter Certificate constituted a permanent teaching license.

A little of this I already knew, as I had visited the local District School Board in November, and gleaned some idea of how complex the system was. They had said that once I received the Letter, I should return to their office to begin following through. Having received it just in time for the ringing out of the old year and ringing in of the new, I decided to follow up a few days later.

But before Mike and Ari returned to Jamaica, we had to take a critical step in a more urgent plan. I wasn't satisfied with the preparation-for-life we had so far been able to give Ari, which would soon leave her on her own with only the professional bargaining power of a Jamaican Teachers' College Diploma. Most teachers were quite low paid in Jamaica, and those without degrees were naturally paid less.

If Ari should ever wish to apply for residence in Canada, she would have an enormous challenge saving, on her salary, for the application requirements. Also, her teaching diploma would not be a marketable qualification in Canada, which meant that she probably would not qualify for admission. Furthermore, Ari was unique among her siblings, in ways that suggested she would be well served by another year of our close family support.

I had discovered the Canadian Montessori Academy, and investigated the training programs they offer. In one academic year of intense training that included several months of minimum wage paid internship, Ari could upgrade her qualification to an Associate Degree in Montessori early childhood education. Our initial outlay would be $7,500 Canadian, paid between January and June, but she could recover some of it through the internship stipend. When she returned to Jamaica at the end of the course, the new qualification would place her in a higher wage bracket at local Montessori and other private schools. Whenever she finally decided to apply for Canadian residence, it would be with a Canadian qualification that was marketable in the private education sector here.

All this information had been relayed to Mike and Ari in Jamaica, and I had made contact on Ari's behalf with the Academy. The next step was for her to apply. As she wouldn't be available for the interviews normally scheduled later, she also wished to be interviewed by the administrator while she was here on holiday. So, a couple of days before she and Mike departed Ottawa, she met with the administrator. With her application process thus started, she could return home well geared to complete it.

When we parted at the Ottawa Airport a couple of days later, it was with a lighter heart than in September. The way forward seemed clearer and the period of separation less indefinite. Sean's wedding had been scheduled for the weekend of our March Break, and the plan was for us to re-gather in Jamaica for that week, after which Mike would return to Canada with us, for good.

Sean and his bride planned to live in what Canadians call the "in-law suite" at our home in the hills, but we all expected that eventually they would want to move down to the city. I wasn't worried about them. A man and his new wife *should* be on their own, and I knew the strength of the three-stranded cord they would form with God. Arianne, about whom I did worry, would also live in the house for a few months, and then, I fully expected, would return to Canada to begin the one-year course of study in July.

January

It had been a great Christmas holiday, and 2001 had dawned bringing even greater expectations. January is a special month in our family, partly by accident and partly by design. Both Mike and I have January birthdays, and we were married in the January that he attained the liberating age of 21, and I, 20. Although this year we would have to celebrate separately, the month still promised exciting landmarks.

The day after Mike and Arianne left, I was back at the District School Board office with my Letter of Eligibility. An officer there retained the original, explained the aspects of their employment process that were still gray areas to me, and handed me a stack of information. I now understood that one had no choice but to supply-teach for a while, before entertaining the hope of being offered a position in a public school. The District Board administered the supply system for the region's public schools, and they would issue me an Employee Identification Number (EIN) in due course. In my hands they placed lists of area schools, maps, addresses, contact information for school administrators, a logbook for recording sessions of substitute teaching, and a couple of forms to be completed and returned.

On one form, I should indicate my preferences of geographical area. The District Board provided their schools with a list of available supply teachers, and each year's list was revised only in March. As my name would not yet appear on it, I was advised to visit as many schools as possible, introduce myself and advertise my pending availability. As soon as I got the EIN and was called in for the first full day of supply teaching, I should come back to the District Board with my log book duly signed, and they would return my completed Letter of Eligibility to the OCT.

So, there was still a far way to go, but at least I was on the road. At home, I spread the OC Transpo map on the floor, selected those sections of the city that were within an hour's reach by bus, and listed the elementary schools in these areas. Then, there was a stack of letters and résumés to be prepared, as well as telephone calls to be made. Finally, there were the visits, which really gave a lot of practice commuting through mid-winter conditions.

By then, I was happy to walk in shallow snow for the traction it provides, and learning how to manage a slippery slide on an icy strip. But I wasn't happy walking past snow banks higher than my head. Couldn't they fall on you? And I wasn't happy side-stepping a pile-up left in the path by the snow plow, only to trip and end up on all-fours in it. You think *you* are in *it*, till you get up, brush yourself off and realize that *the snow is in your bag, your boots and the folds of your clothing.*

And it's not inviting to step off a bus into a bank that is knee deep. You get accustomed to looking for footprints into which to step. This works fine, unless there is freezing water at the bottom of the holes. But all of this could be chalked up to novelty, and recounted as adventure stories, except that one was trying to arrive at a school office looking as presentable as possible.

The reception everywhere was very polite, and a couple of vice principals made helpful suggestions for my continuing quest. When I received the EIN, I should phone it in, they said, and they would add me to their list. However, there was a private school to which I had applied in December[3], and after an interview there, the vice-principal promised to place me on his 2000 list of supply teachers. I offered him a couple of hours per week of volunteer service, to continue familiarizing myself with the Canadian classroom, in preparation for being "called out" to substitute. The volunteering at this school began in January, replacing the service at the public school near Chief Cousin's house. The commission sales work continued, but very low key. So, although unemployed, I was out as often as I could face the bone-chilling wind.

I became literally afraid of the cold that met me outside the front door, even for the time it took to bring in the morning paper. The first few breaths I would take, usually brought a fit of coughing. After that, it was OK, except that the kids complained when we were out together that I walked too fast. A toque (called a "tam" in Jamaica) was always pulled down over my ears, and I lived in turtle-neck sweaters because I didn't like fussing with scarves.

Sometimes, the neck of the sweater was unfolded and stretched up over my lips.

It dawned on me that lipstick must have been invented in a cold country, for protection. I never had much use for make-up before, but suddenly, lipstick and some more slick over it were absolute necessities. I was sorry I couldn't plaster it as far as the laugh lines, for the need didn't really stop with the lips.

My nose froze repeatedly, and was always runny. So, I took every precaution to avoid becoming the spectacle I had observed one day—a person with an icicle hanging from the nose. After the first time my ears froze, I never let it happen again. It was too scary; they felt like two pieces of board at the sides of my face. I went through several pairs of inexpensive gloves, sometimes

---

3. See Appendix, letter to Home Church brethren in Jamaica and the US, of January 8, 2000, 6:23 a.m., section "# 7"

wearing them over each other, or inside of mittens, and still my fingers were icy. One day I stopped at a store, and after peeling off the gloves, my fingers refused to grip the zipper of my purse. To add insult to injury, my mouth was too frozen to coherently explain to the cashier what was taking so long.

The first two coats I bought were not good choices. One was long but had no hood, and the other had a hood, but was short. By the time I discovered the gravity of this shopping mistake, I couldn't afford to buy another. Once or twice, I actually wore them together, and felt like a stuffed (but warm) owl.

One of my biggest fears in coming to Canada was that the intermittent joint pains I had so far tried to ignore would worsen. Thank God, that didn't happen to the extent that I had feared. Only my knees told me when it was just too cold. They didn't scream at me; they just whispered the occasional scolding, like, "You know you should have worn that long coat today!" Despite all of this, it took a long time to form the habit of listening to the weather forecast before dressing to leave the house. Eventually, I learnt when to augment the thermal underwear, thick socks and heavy clothing with a particular choice of outer protection.

The private school did call me in for a couple of days in January, and while that brought a welcome check, it didn't count toward the OCT's requirements. Finally, on Friday the 28th, I was called in for the afternoon session at the public school where I had first volunteered. Between these first two instances, I earned only $319.73 from teaching in January, but it was a start.

Chapter 14

"OC Transpo"

Public use of urban transit and intercity carriers declined slightly in 1998, after an increase of 21 billion (in passengers carried) between 1995 and 1997. 1998 industry expenditure on urban transit and school buses was $4,481.8 million, and revenue was $5,412 million.[1]

My first jottings on OC Transpo were made way back in September '99, and regular reliance on the bus company's services kept the growing file fresh in my mind. In Jamaica we had very little to compare with it; in fact I would have been severely limited without a car back home. Jamaican public transportation was by comparison under-funded, unreliable, uncomfortable, unsafe, and worse in 1999 than when I relied on it as an energetic youth. Before coming to Canada I had been driving for about 20 years, and able to achieve certain goals only because of that.

I was born functionally blind in the left eye. Having grown up with this disability, I compensated enough to drive in Jamaica's left-hand-drive environment, where traffic usually approaches on the right. In Canada, where everything comes at you from the left, I had decided after the first few days to play it safe, and entrust my movements in Ottawa-Carleton to OC Transpo. This was a comfortable decision, because, in my admittedly limited experience, their service seemed very reliable.

---

1.   Adapted from Statistics Canada's Internet Site, http://statcan.ca/english/Pgdb/ Economy/Communications/trade18.htm, August 13, 2002

Over the ensuing months, I would sometimes feel threatened by the weather, and hop on too hurriedly, only to find myself on the wrong bus. At other times, blinded by the frosting on the bus windows, or the weather conditions outside, I would sometimes hop off at the wrong place. Otherwise, it was easy to get to one's destination on a predictable schedule. I soon discovered the significance of the numbers on each bus stop sign or shelter. They were call numbers that (if you had a cell phone or a call box nearby) would get you the time that the next bus would stop there. At a bus stop served by several routes, one then had the choice of which bus and which connections to utilize, in response to time and weather constraints.

Something to Write Home About

In the very first letter I wrote home to the school community in the Blue Mountains, half of it extolled the virtues of OC Transpo. From the efficient driver-ductor[2] with ticket machine at the front, to the freely issued schedule and route brochures, to the blessed "lost and found" system which could help you recover a precious item, to the external color coding that distinguished it from Quebec-destined buses even before the number came into focus: I was impressed. So apparently, were many others over the years of OC Transpo's history. In a June 2000 conference on Urban Visions for Transportation, Transport Minister David Collennete commented that OC Transpo's award winning bus service was attracting more and more riders every year, and its Transitway being used as a model for transit as far away as Brisbane, Australia.[3] Of course, it wasn't long before I experienced their inevitable (human) fallibility, heard the comments of locals who remember better service, and read of the company's April 1999 work-place shooting tragedy. This was being rehashed in January–February 2000, as Ottawa's news media covered the inquest, which highlighted industrial relations problems within the company's ranks, as well as the case history of a company mechanic-turned-shooter.

Excused by suicide from the inquest, the shooter missed his emerging profile as a marijuana user and inadequately treated psychotic. The undercurrent of resentment against Francophones that was drawing much comment in Ottawa, where Quebec is only a bridge away, had reportedly

---

2.   "Ductor"–Jamaican slang for "conductor"

3.   Transport   Canada's   website,   http://www.tc.gc.ca/mediaroom/ speeches/2000/000603e-fcm.htm

fuelled his "persecution complex," as had on-the-job teasing about his suspect wash-room habits.

With all of the bad publicity, my appreciation of OC Transpo was not severely altered. Though twice as expensive (one way) as public transportation between Kingston and some nearby Blue Mountain districts, it earned the complement expressed by Louise Bennett's line, "i' wut i'."[4] Besides, within the almost two hours covered by the "transfer" ticket, one could often conclude the business of the trip and embark on a pre-paid return journey.

Deborah, who used to suffer stoically on the after-school bus route along Kingston's Hope Road to Papine, announced one day, "You know Mummy, I really love this bus system!" Usually, the bus was on time, and we all appreciated this pattern. On occasion, however, it was late, to the chagrin of commuters heading for work or other appointments. I recall a college student stewing next to me in a bus shelter on Carling, verbalising all her fears of being fired from her part time job. Of course, she wasn't Canadian—for Canadian youth don't usually talk much to strangers.

Then, one Saturday, the 118 to Kanata that was due at Baseline and Clyde at 11:02, totally failed to appear. Not until the next scheduled time of 11:32 did a bus grace the horizon. The driver said there had been a breakdown. Frustrated at the prospect of being late for two appointments down the line, I mentally rejected that excuse. As if accustomed to such reliability, I fumed inwardly that a bus should have been sent from wherever, to fill in.

Good, Bad and Indifferent Drivers

Apart from a printed schedule and general punctuality, another welcome difference from Jamaican public transportation was the usually cordial manner of the drivers. Most responded politely to a greeting or query, and were very helpful to commuters—even those whose accents they found unfamiliar. And if you disembarked at the front door (which you were not really supposed to do) some would send you off with a cheery, "Have a good day, now!" I even heard a particular driver greet each ascending passenger individually, at every stop, on a slow afternoon.

The drivers' occasional waiting at bus stops for people from connecting routes, or simply to fulfil the specifics of their schedule, was also very

---

4.   Jamaican Creole meaning, "It's worth the price", from poem of the same title in: *Jamaica Labrish* by Louise Bennett.

comforting. I wished these courtesies were practised by all the drivers all the time, especially regarding the schedule.

In the chill of winter, and where there was no shelter, it seemed cruel for a bus to pass by earlier than the scheduled time, since some commuters would have timed their arrival at the bus stop to minimise exposure.

Of course, we did get the grumpy ones—like the one who looked away and kept his mouth shut as if he hadn't heard my greeting. Well, I hadn't been a teacher for 19 years for nothing. In the way of one teaching manners to an infant, I simply repeated it more deliberately and with more exaggerated pleasantness. And, of course, he thought better of it and answered me.

There were also the odd drivers who looked straight at you rushing to get the bus, and drove by or moved off. I even saw a driver making a big fuss one afternoon, against an Asian man who had boarded with his infant in a stroller, and sat with it drawn up against his legs at the front of the bus. Had I not seen similar carriages happily accommodated in that very position before, I would perhaps have swallowed the driver's claim that it shouldn't be there. But it was either that other drivers had bent the rules, (which they perhaps shouldn't have done) or that he had something personal against this Asian, or that he was just being a grouch.

Long before the media coverage of the OC Transpo inquest began, I had heard another grouch behind the wheel beefing against the company's policies, which he claimed resulted in unnecessary mechanical breakdowns and employee discontent. His comments, perhaps valid and directed toward a specific passenger, were inappropriately audible to many, and I found it an unpleasant start to the ride.

How quickly I had become accustomed to peace and quiet on a bus! How far removed from the blaring, dance-hall "music" to which passengers in Jamaica were often a captive audience! I also appreciated the reservation of front seats for people with special needs, with the fingertip buzzers on handrails, padded siding, and priority placement next to the door. Especially in this neutered, un-chivalrous age—the pregnant, the elderly, or the unwell might otherwise have to strain against acceleration to avoid falling into the laps of the seated able-bodied.

I often thought, though, that people like me, who didn't know exactly where they were going, may also need to be at the front of the bus, to read approaching road signs in good time. Most drivers were quite good at helping passengers to get off at the right place, but it was also reassuring to keep track of exactly where you were, intersection by intersection. One way around this was the too infrequent practice of drivers loudly naming approaching intersections. I imagined that it could be tedious, but in a city teeming with immigrants it was a rare and welcome sound.

An eye-opener for me was OC Transpo's special provision for the disabled: automatic lifts at the front doors of some buses, and their special, Para-Transpo vehicles, which served persons unable to use the regular buses.

"If these special provisions are common in first-world public transportation," I thought, "then excuse my ignorance and take a bow, all ye developed nations. After all, you could have kept the money out of wide circulation rather than using some of it on behalf of these special people."

Routes and Passengers

My first exposure to OC Transpo was the number 3 route to and from Nepean Centre at the start of the school year. One initial, rose-tinted observation was how clean the bus shelters were. However, as the semester moved into full swing, some high-schoolers succeeded in changing that, and I formed certain opinions of the school populations based on the conditions of "their" bus shelters.

I also concluded that winter has an adverse effect on the shelters, though I couldn't figure out why. Was it just the supreme preoccupation with escaping the chill, and relieving its oppressive mindset, which resulted in litter not only multiplying inside the shelter, but muck being sprayed onto the walls as well?

You guessed it: I'm squeamish. No matter what the wind-chill factor, I couldn't happily take refuge very close to a windshield splattered with drools of what looked dangerously like frozen sputum. The first time I saw it was at Baseline and Guthrie, but in short order, it began turning up in other places, apparently the work of more than one prankster.

Vandalism would have been too harsh a word, as presumably the defacement could be washed off. But the word came to mind as I recalled seeing, early in my OC Transpo exposure, a notice in a bus shelter offering a reward for information on bus-shelter vandalism. That was a wonderfully new concept to me (rewards in serious criminal investigations is what I'm used to) but did anyone ever bother to rattle?

Reading seemed a favorite past-time on the buses. Some passengers pulled out their choice of literature the minute they settled in their seats. But some youngsters chatted up a storm, usually in the back. No problem at all—fine with me, in fact—except when they started to swear. Obscene or profane language jerks my chain. In Jamaica, the insane were the only ones who used to spew profanity without provocation; although bar room talk and the street language of sexual harassment could get quite colorful. Others would hardly swear except in quarrelling, and even then, upbringing usually dictated alternative responses.

With the influence of Hollywood, things were changing, but this incorporation of obscenities into casual conversation was something I had never heard before, except in movies. I thought Hollywood exaggerated the role of profanity in its portrayal of daily life, just for the box office effect of catering to man's appetite for forbidden fruit. Shortly before leaving Jamaica at the age of 45, I walked out of a movie because the swearing was almost literally hurting my ears. I told the concerned clerk in the lobby that I was "much too young" for this movie, and declined her offer of entry into the next cinema. It seemed too big a risk.

But here, every so often one was pounded by foul-mouthed teenagers in the bus. If it didn't let up, I tried to move out of earshot. Otherwise, I wrestled with the impulse to chide them. One can't go to Rome and tell the Romans how to behave, can one? But the day came that the orator was standing right over my head, and the bus was crowded. When I couldn't take it anymore, I looked directly up at him and said, "Excuse me, young man. Watch your language, please!"

I think he was stunned. He actually apologised, and for a blissful while it had the desired effect. But before I was safely off the bus, he and his friend were at it again. Was this a vocabulary problem? When I spoke with more seasoned Jamaican immigrants about this kind of thing, they said I was lucky to be only hearing it on the bus routes. When I got a job, they said, I would likely realize that it's common parlance, even in the workplace.

Oh, For Truly Fume-free Commuting!

Another problem with bussing was the inconsiderate habits of some smokers. Occasionally, I had to remain outside the shelter, in the cold, to avoid second-hand smoke from nicotine users. These were young Canadians, so I nursed the hope that they would eventually conform to the civility of their elders, which has institutionalised the protection of non-smokers.

Then there was the spitting. What was it with these people who seemed bent on splattering the floor with their unwanted saliva? In winter it set like freezing rain; but frozen or not, it had me mincing steps within the shelter, and wondering why on earth they didn't spit outside. My mother used to tell tales from her study period in England of the 1950's, and it was apparently a serious misdemeanor there to spit in public places. Different age, different country, different commuters.

In a particular incident that aroused more pity than annoyance, two schoolboys sharing a smoke left the bus shelter empty as they saw me approaching, and went to finish their treat huddled together against the wind, some distance away. The first breath I took inside the shelter told me their cigarette was marijuana, a "ganja spliff" as we Jamaicans call it.

I recognised its pungency from exposure to pockets of users in the Blue Mountains, where I would drive very quickly through the nocturnal festivities at a particular village square, or sometimes stand outside the buying station where I went to sell our coffee beans, just to avoid the "weed's" pollution. My pity for these Nepean students stemmed from my conviction, formed through personal observation of students during those years, that marijuana is an even greater danger to the brain than nicotine is to the lungs.

Smoking seems to be an epidemic in Canada, as does beer addiction. Fortunately, all public buildings are no-smoking domains; but to see the smokers huddled together outside their workplaces in the biting cold, just to consume cigarettes, is pitiful. "Does it make them feel warm?" I wondered.

It was very informative to listen to locals asserting that OC Transpo service used to be better. The company published their lengthy proposals for improvement in 2000, in press releases aimed at regaining ratings lost. But my overall impression had been positive, and I had learned more complimentary than negative things about the traditional Canadian way of life, just from travelling by bus.[5]

---

5.   For more on OC Transpo, see Appendix (letter to Assistant Teachers at the mission school, dated October 20, 1999).

Chapter 15

Eyes to See, Ears to Hear

"Whatever affects one directly, affects all indirectly. I can never be what I ought to be until you are what you ought to be. This is the interrelated structure of reality."—Martin Luther King Jr.

A Jamaican reader may judge me as being "too faass,"[1] from some of the observations I made riding the buses of OC Transpo. The rebuttal would be that my eyes see, my ears hear, and my brain is bent on making associations. On top of that, my heart has a soft spot for Homo sapiens, and keeps picking the brain as to how they tick.

The first few months that we lived in Nepean, it was a relief not to see as many mentally ill persons on the street as there were in Kingston. On the other hand, I heard of the winter blues that some people get here, and concluded that we tropical people should value our sun a bit more than we do. Sunlight gets taken for granted when your main problem is to find the shade. But even before the end of the fall, I had seen enough in Ottawa to know that the real darkness doesn't always wait for winter.

One day, in November, a teenage girl had jumped onto the bus on Somerset, anxiously followed as far as the door by a very concerned man in late mid-life, who asked her a couple of times whether she was all right. After a few seconds there, he stepped backwards onto the sidewalk, in the face of her brusque response. This could have been just a bout in a parent-teen problem, and the driver was patient in allowing the man a few moments to decide

---

1.   Jamaican Creole meaning "inquisitive, nosy, minding other people's business"

whether he was coming or going. My mind moved on, till we turned onto Bank. I realized that the girl had got off, and was visibly vacillating between going north or south, with her hand fluttering about her face, lips trembling, tears streaming down her cheeks, and an expression of total panic around her eyes. That was not the look of a rebellious but coping teen. I prayed for her till I got off at Albert.

While some passengers read on the buses, I studied the glimpses of life displayed in the relative stillness. Body piercings at close range were most interesting. Eyebrow rings, nose rings, and lip rings vied for prominence, sometimes on the face of the same teenager. Earrings had migrated far north of the lobe, protruding through every available millimetre of the part God thought He had so well sculptured and stiffened with cartilage. To get those holes up there must have been a crunchy effort. But the intrigue of the tongue rings took the cake! As the wearer inevitably lolled his or her tongue about, playing with it, I tried to figure out the structure and limitations of the contraption. Unlike the others, it was always a knob. Wasn't it torturous to have it installed in the first place? Did they use a topical dressing on the wound, and was there antibiotic intake involved in the aftermath of these piercings? Did they take it out at nights? How many of these things got accidentally swallowed?

The importance of make-up in this society also began to dawn on me, as I occasionally watched females come on to the bus, take out their kits and mirrors, and unhurriedly do what they presumably had no time to do at home. Layer by layer, sometimes eyelash by eyelash, they worked at enhancing nature's endowment; totally oblivious to anyone's scrutiny. I think I was the only one looking, anyway, and finding this public preening a very educational novelty. So that's how it was done! (As if I needed to know.)

The Lord God Made Us All

When my thoughts weren't falling prey to such trivia, I mused on more important observations. One was the difference between client services in Jamaica and here in Canada. In the area of social services, there seems nothing to be gained from good "customer service" (except a measure of public contentment and perhaps political stability). Nevertheless, I noted that respect, provision and care for the society's weakest links were evidently built into Canadian life and politics. And it was meted out with all the charm accorded to paying customers in a commercial setting.

People still slipped through the cracks, but this seemed to be the exception and not the rule. The mentally ill, the physically disabled, and the aged were helped to remain where possible in the mainstream, at best being as productive as anyone else, and at worst being cherished reminders of man's frailty. Motorised wheelchairs moved along sidewalks, through pedestrian crossings, in and out of buildings as briskly as the stream of feet. Of the few beggars I had seen, not one was physically disabled. And the disabled were not ridiculed or openly abused, even by children. Their integration with the able-bodied, piloted in Jamaican education at Kingston's Hope Valley Experimental School, was seen in full bloom here. The developmentally delayed were taught as much of practical life skills as they could absorb, so many of them commuted by bus unaccompanied. Their often strange conversation was accepted and responded to as politely as anyone else's, and harmless eccentricities passed without comment. As a curious newcomer, I marvelled at how the tics and benign behaviours caused no stir on the buses. The sufferers even seemed trained that they should use the designated seating at the front of the bus. Only once did I see a man who should obviously have been there, sitting elsewhere. He was perched restlessly on the edge of a seat near the back, muttering plaintively, "We don't have a boy... we don't have a boy..."

The mentally challenged were generally so well cared for that they could pass unnoticed. I remember the lady who came to the door during our orientation period at Chief Cousin's house, asking for food and drink. Deb dutifully went to prepare a snack, in wide-eyed wonder that there were beggars in Canada too. Only when she returned to deliver it, did she suspect the lady was more mentally than gastro-intestinally affected, for she had wandered off aimlessly without the food. About a week later, she was back, became slightly aggressive, and demanded a tour of the kitchen. This time Claire gently returned her to the door to await some refreshment.

Then, there was the stranger who turned up at a well publicised dinner hosted by Chief Cousin's church. He selected our table, and informed the rest of us that he had just signed himself temporarily out of a psychiatric ward, to attend the function. Except for the persistent tic, the bandage on his arm from an intravenous attachment, and his obsessive prattle about a book he was compiling (on fellow war heroes), he was almost the perfect dinner guest. He had actually brought the bulky manuscript with him, and it did seem an interesting project, but this was neither the place nor the time. If he found the response less than enthusiastic, he magnanimously ignored it, for his grandiose plans needed no-one's acceptance.

In this climate of provision for the disabled, I even came to the brink of trying to milk my visual impairment. Desperately in need of employment, I responded to Walmart's advertised program to train and employ disabled workers. Their telephone representative agreed that I qualified to apply; but when I attended the first orientation meeting, and saw other applicants with much more obvious degrees of physical and mental disability, some attended by professionals responsible for them, my conscience said, loud and clear, "Evangeline, what's wrong with this picture? You have never before tried to profiteer from that eye. Don't start now!" So I resolved to wait for the next employment opportunity.

It may be unfair of me to compare provisions for the disabled here and in Jamaica—as unfair as it may be for the Smiths' children to resent their parents for not providing them with what the Jones' children have. But, imagine the Smith children's justifiable thoughts if they observe their parents spending lavishly on themselves, while meeting the children's needs with claims of being empty-pocketed.

We know that money can't provide love or things eternal, but it can certainly be used very convincingly to demonstrate caring concern. It can even make the environment safer for the "more fortunate," by enhancing the contentment and coping mechanisms of the "less fortunate." I wish some Third World millionaires and politicians were not such selfish, short-sighted stewards of their fortunes and public funds. They themselves would live longer.

February

On Tuesday, February 1, I did the second half-day of supply teaching at the school where I had first volunteered. That completed the requirements for my Letter of Eligibility to be signed and returned by the District Board to the OCT. But I wasn't called in again for the whole month of February. The schools were working with their September edition of the supply teacher list, and if anyone had actually tacked my name on to the end, apparently they never got that far down the list in calling around for substitutes.

Working on my own list, I completed the visits to area schools, and the phoning in of my EIN[2] to update the earlier information. I still worked at the advertising sales job, but since our outlay on the house, Mike had begun to cover most of our expenses by money transfers from Jamaica.

I applied to a private after-school learning centre for part time work, but nothing came of that within the month. There was no boredom, however, and only brief lapses into worry, for I wrung contentment out of researching and writing a Christian column in the secular, monthly tabloid for which I sold advertisements.

After 30 years of sporadically contributing to various publications, I felt honored to be a regular columnist with an established paper. The publication principally served an ethnic rather than a geographical community, so I also felt blessed with the opportunity for Christian influence among its target readership. Though fully committed to the human rights aspect of Canada's multiculturalism, the publisher / editor also believed that Christianity should not be trampled underfoot of the fast arriving world religions. So, in this secular publication, he tried to maintain that peculiar flavour; and I was one of two columnists who sprinkled the salt.

This had started in October, with ideas that had gushed from a long dammed reservoir, and been fuelled by current events as I soaked up the media coverage of Canadian life and outlook. Here, we had not only the secular dailies, but Christian papers too, published fortnightly or monthly. A successful, regular Christian newspaper is something to which many Jamaicans had looked forward.[3] The ones I discovered here seemed representative of mainstream Canadian Christian commentary. They also supplemented the reports of the dailies with important news that had either escaped their notice, or their grasp of relevance.

Lifestyle Changes

At home, we settled into a comfortable, new routine. Deb and Joe had always relied on someone else to do the bulk of the housework they created. In Jamaica, it had been the full-time "helper" and Mummy who picked up after them and did most of the shopping, cooking, cleaning and laundry. At Chief Cousin's, where we occupied relatively little space and Mummy was at home

---

2.   Employee Identification Number
3.   See "Finally..." in Chapter 19.

a lot, they had still escaped much housework. But now, a roster on the wall called the shots.

2 Thessalonians 3:10 was growing teeth in synch with the development of their late molars. "If any would not work, neither should he eat," (KJV). Deb and Joe agreed in principle, but it took some persistent monitoring to replace old habits with new, and eliminate the convenient "forgetting" of duties. Furthermore, we didn't see eye to eye on the need for certain things. Ironing was one, and I accepted after a while that compromise was needed there.

But my impaired vision was like 20/20 compared to their normal perception of a mess, and here there was very little compromise. It's probably pathological, but I hate a mess. Furniture, as I understand it, is designed to keep other things off the floor. And even with our sparse furnishings, there was designated storage for most things. Why should drawers be empty when bins were overflowing with clean but crumpled clothes? Why should boot trays be bare when shoes were parked north, south, east and west of them? It beat me, and since I could no longer spank, or devote much time to devising elaborate motivational schemes, I used my volume and tone vocal options a lot.

Garbage disposal, Canadian style, was a learning experience. In Jamaica, there was no recycling required for garbage collection in the cities, and rural dwellers often disposed of their own garbage in a number of ways. Our method had been to burn paper and flammable trash, dump the bio-degradable into a compost hole, and bag the rest for deposit into a city dumpster on one of our frequent trips down the mountain.

So, we had grown accustomed to dual garbage containers in the kitchen, but the precision in sorting and packaging for disposal that we learnt from Claire was a step ahead. The city provided householders with color coded "boxes" (hard plastic bins) in which to put out plastic, glass and metal products separately from paper products. Each category was collected fortnightly, and if the wrong box were put out on a specific day, it would be left untouched. Only the "yucky" garbage was bagged, and could be put out weekly. Leaves and other garden waste were collected in specific bags sold in the supermarkets, and large tree cuttings could be tied in bundles and placed on the sidewalk on seasonally designated collection days.

I won't say we folded and compressed the cartons as meticulously as Claire did, but with everything else we did a fair job, and in our new location the processing of garbage became a Sunday evening family chore.

Doing their share of the cooking and dish washing was the easiest part for Deb and Joe. Very little here had to be prepared from scratch, compared with our mountain home, where, years ago, we had even butchered chickens and pigs with the help of farm hands. And in Jamaica, the dish washing had already been rostered among everyone in the house, but without the luxury of a dishwasher.

Mike was the real gourmet, and without him there were less specifications to be met in meal preparation. I had grasped the opportunity for healthier eating since we arrived in Canada, feasting on a much wider variety of fresh fruit and vegetables than we were able to afford in Jamaica. Deb and Joe consumed more unhelpful stuff, but I figured their dawn of reason would eventually come.

More of School

Ontario's public "elementary and secondary schools are administered by District School Boards, the oldest form of publicly elected government in Ontario. Working within the framework of the Education Act and its regulations, district school boards adapt provincial education policy to local situations."[4]

At Chief Cousin's, the kids had been given two dysfunctional bicycles that Joe had repaired. With these, they rode to school when the weather was good. Otherwise, they walked. By the time we moved, they had settled fully into the life of that school and were doing very well. So, I wrote to the proper authority (principal of the new area school), for a waiver on the requirement that they should change schools to attend one nearer to their new address. These kids were still in transition in so many ways, I argued, that switching schools now would definitely be detrimental to their emotional and scholastic progress.

The authorities sanctioned their retention at the school, and we added the cost of monthly student bus passes (roughly $100) to our budget. At school, life had become even more interesting. Joe's gym teacher had recruited him to the school's wrestling team, and with a couple of months' training he looked the part. Amused as I was with the singlet he wore for tournaments, his

---

4. Ontario Ministry of Education Internet Site, http://www.edu.gov.on.ca/eng/ general/elemsec/es_overview.html,
   August 13, 2002

bulging body looked too scandalous in it, so I never took a picture. Perhaps I just needed a bit more exposure.

But, before we could get that, the dangers of the sport began to manifest themselves, and I became the masseuse shopping for soothing embrocations and joint wraps. Sean had put me through this before, when he served a couple of seasons on his high school track and field team. So, I just sighed, kneaded, and wrapped. Fortunately, we didn't have to ice-pack. But then, I had a nightmare that wouldn't leave my mind. I saw this woman lamenting the death or serious injury of her son in a wrestling match, and the woman wasn't me. It seemed she was the mother of Joe's opponent. I started to pray him out of the sport. At the next tournament he got thrown so badly, and came home with such a sore neck and shoulder, that he decided to quit.

Meanwhile, Deb's leadership potential had attracted the scrutiny of staff members, who nominated her for the school's annual Leadership Camp. Very flattering, but again I had to go shopping, this time for camping gear. Hiking to Blue Mountain Peak had never required all this, but we dutifully combed the shelves of Canadian Tire till we had the requirements. Then, we proudly sent her off, and it proved a good time for bonding with key players in the school community.

February brought the end of the semester, the second report card, and another round of parent-teacher conferences. Although I looked hard at the grades and pressed my own evaluation at home, the teachers were even more complimentary now about the kid's conduct and participation in classes. When wonder was expressed at their co-operation and other teacher-valued attitudes, I failed my own test as the obvious comment stopped at my throat. They had been brought up in the nurture *and admonition* of the Lord! Shame on me for withholding that!

Birds of similar plumage are not necessarily of the same stock. This seemed clear as I watched the formation of friendships among Deb, Joe and their peers. The shared immigrant experience was one common factor, though the growing group included only one other Jamaican. Other factors that attracted were religious upbringing, similar concepts of decency, and similar family values. Those that repelled were foul language, vulgarity, and disdain of godliness. The result was a small group of Christians, Muslims and others, who became friends despite the incompatibility of their doctrines, or their religious ambivalence. I wondered, how long would these birds of similar but essentially different feather be able to flock together, and in what direction would they fly?

Chapter 16

Spring, Summer...

Canada's coldest city is Yellowknife (North West Territories), with a mean annual temperature of–5.4° C. The warmest city is Vancouver (British Columbia), mean annual temperature 10.4° C.[1]

Mummy often told a funny story about my nursery school recitation, part of which went like this: "The *four* seasons of the year are spring, summer, autumn and winter!" Knowing that all we see of weather changes in Jamaica are rainy, dry and hurricane seasons, she asked me, "What are seasons?"

Already the know-it-all at three, I looked at her incredulously and replied, "*Counting!*" As the Ottawa winter of 1999– 2000 wore on, I often thought that Mummy would have had a good laugh if she could have witnessed my reactions to the first experience of the real thing. Just as Chief Cousin had predicted, before February was over we were all longing for spring. Then, March began to warm very slowly, the snow-banks gradually shrinking into reservoirs of ugly, grey slush.

I was only called out to supply in public schools for three and a half days in March, but did a couple more at the private school where I was also volunteering. By the middle of the month, there was also a firm offer of part-time employment with the learning centre to which I had applied. This learning centre was almost at the other end of the city. The counterparts close to home had no openings for me. Scheduling would be tricky, as I still had to reserve most of the day for the public schools' infrequent calls. It would

---

1.   Readers Digest Atlas of Canada, 1995, p. 50

go against me, I had been told, if I were unavailable when a call did come in. So, we set a schedule for evening work, which allowed me over an hour to commute.

As the learning centre was just opening, I worked only a few hours at the very end of March. The District Board paid $21.*903 (that's what the slip says!)* per hour, the private day school a bit less, and the after-school learning centre only $15 per hour. By hey, it all adds up—much better than sitting at home, awaiting the perfect, tailor-made job.

I still converted Canadian prices into Jamaican dollar equivalents at 1:26 to judge value, and tried in vain to get Deb and Joe to do the same. (Each snack they downed at a measly 99c plus tax was actually $30 worth of little more than sugar!) As long as we were depleting our tiny Jamaican dollar nest egg, we'd have to think of it that way. Why was the import of this so hard to grasp?

Back home, preparations were in full swing for Sean's wedding. Except for some shopping done in Ottawa and shipped home in January, I had escaped Scot free from the associated labours. Mike was the one involved as much as this groom's parents needed to be. My task before we joined them in mid-March was to purchase a vehicle, as Mike would return to Ottawa with us in the final week of the month and start a full-time job on April 1.

He would need a vehicle for this job, and was reluctant to wait till he could shop for it himself. It should be a van, as we also anticipated visits from family, and wanted at least a seven-seater. As Chief Cousin and I made the rounds of car dealerships over a couple of weeks, I discovered that many Canadians lease rather than purchase their vehicles, because they find the financing for that easier to manage. I relayed all the information to Mike, but he wanted to purchase. Finally, we settled on a good deal with a manageable deposit and a one-year moratorium on payments. This time wonder of wonders—the institutions approved our credit application without what I had begun to regard as the inevitable fuss.

Six Months to the Day

On March 11, Deb, Joe and I happily hopped onto a plane for a week-long break from chilly Ottawa. We had been here six months to the day. Six hours later, as we drove through Kingston, it seemed we had left only yesterday. The amusing thing was that I felt compelled to buy some of my favorite patties before starting up the Blue Mountain to our home. We had actually been without real patties for long enough! In Ottawa, we could buy boxes of frozen substitutes labeled "Tastee," but they went soggy in the microwave, too crisp in the oven, and the taste didn't come close to the Jamaican Tastee product, let alone my choice variety.

By the end of a very short week, I had packed the household effects we could afford to have shipped to Ottawa, and Mike had got them to the shippers. There were books, crockery, photographs, favorite artwork and decorator items. The only furniture we took was a beautiful, mahogany corner table that Mike had inherited, and a Caribbean-styled set of lounge chairs. Their colorful upholstery would definitely redeem the monotony of Ottawa's neutral tones. The rocking love-seat built by Mike's grandfather had to be left behind, with all the other things I knew I would miss.

The house was still adequately furnished, for Arianne would be there till June, and then it would be rented as it was. A new chairperson had been appointed to the board of the mission school, and an educator from our church in Kingston was preparing to take over from the expatriate acting principal. This new principal was arranging with us to rent part of the house, and the care of the coffee farm was being turned over to a trusted employee and her husband. The furnished in-law suite was locked off "for Anderson use"—a home base where any of our scattered tribe could touch down when necessary. Mike was loathe to relinquish occupancy of the entire property, for that spelt a burning of convenient bridges.

On Saturday morning, Deb and Joe made their debut as bridesmaid and best-man, Arianne made hers as wedding poet, and Gail's crescendos rang out in a wedding duet with a musical friend. The next day, our newly-weds having departed for a famed, Jamaican honeymoon, we headed once more for Norman Manley Airport. Gail had more time before she was scheduled to return to the US; so, she and her friend drove us to the airport.

Mike was traveling on a complimentary ticket (a "buddy pass" donated by a friend) and we were grateful for that, although it meant he was on standby while the rest of us were confirmed for the flight. On this particular Sunday afternoon, North American youth at the end of their March Break had begun to head home in droves. Very soon, it became clear that Mike might not get a seat on our flight after all. The airline agents at Norman Manley were very sympathetic. Finally, they advised that if we wished to take the chance, Mike could certainly travel with us to Montego Bay, the tourist resort town where some passengers would be disembarking and others embarking. There, it would become clear whether he could continue on the flight.

He had to get off with his hand luggage at "Mo-Bay" without knowing whether or not he would be "bumped". He decided that if he was, he would return to Kingston and bunk with his mother while awaiting the first available flight out. We kissed each other goodbye, with me "declaring in faith" that he would be back in his seat shortly. This "faith" turned out to be presumption and wishful thinking; for in short order, the plane, full to capacity, took off without him.

In the wee hours of Monday morning, we three arrived in Ottawa, lugging baggage for four. Chief Cousin, the faithful, was at the airport to pick us up. Bright-eyed, cheery and welcoming, he leaned over his tummy to bless each of us with his characteristic embrace, kissing first on one cheek and then on the other. He had come in our new van, which had been parked at his home for the week.

Spring and New Life

It was not till Thursday that Mike could get on a flight for Ottawa. He wasted no time, however; as there were still loose ends we would have had to tie up by mail, which he took the opportunity to deal with in person. So, the delay became a boon to this stage of our peculiar migration process. Here was a reminder for us of where faith should be placed—in God's promise "that all things work together for good to them that love God, to them who are the called according to His purpose."[2]

For the rest of March, I was called out for two half-days of supply teaching, and Mike continued to search the job market for anything more promising than the offer he already had. Nothing yielding, he got ready to begin his new job, and started work on Monday, April 3rd. To say that Mike is a hard-working employee is to understate an essential quality about him. From his days as a technician through to his years in management positions, he was the type they make movies about. However, by the grace of God, he wasn't free to pursue unrestrained "the way that seems right to a man, but in the end ... leads to death."[3] I'm a very good restrainer when I put my mind to it, for after all, his demise would not spell well-being for the rest of us.

---

2.   Romans 8: 28, the Bible, King James Version.
3.   Proverbs 14: 12

This new job was a step down the corporate ladder, but edged with divine silver linings. First, Mike regained his physical fitness in due course, after enduring several weeks of backache. As a hobby farmer and self-employed businessman, he had kept trim and sinewy for many years. But, return to management positions with large firms had meant less physical activity and some loss of muscle tone. Now required to do the legwork he had previously supervised from an office, he began to look again like a leaner hunk. Secondly, he got to know Ottawa much faster than he would have with a desk job. He was sometimes sent further afield than I had traveled doing the circuit of schools, and quickly began to overcome the challenges posed by the unfamiliar traffic and road systems. New job skills were the third benefit. The machines he had to service included (surprisingly) older models that the Jamaican branch had been phasing out. Mike was sent to Toronto and Montreal for a few days' training on these.

My little, green logbook shows April to have been a huge improvement over the previous months. I worked for almost half the available hours in public schools, and found that I was getting an encouraging number of calls from a particular one. Increasingly regular, though still insufficient, the hours at the after-school learning centre supplemented my income. If I was called out with enough notice for morning supply work, Mike could sometimes give me a lift. Otherwise, I continued bussing it as before.

My jottings on April 4 record a late call to a school within walking distance of home. I got there, did three-quarters of a day's work, and at 3:20 p.m. got a taxi to the learning centre across town. It cost $23.10 to get there in the nick of time, to earn less than $30.00; so, very often these excursions were more for honor than anything else. The trip home was usually leisurely, and on this particular afternoon, my red-ink pen scrawled disjointed thoughts on the back of a math worksheet I had used with students that day.

> "1/2 hour to Hurdman (bus station) … 18 minutes waiting for the 118 Kanata … sights (through the window)—more greening of grass, less brown showing… The all-day rain has stopped … Daylight saving time since Sunday, so 6 p.m. bright … River running again … mini-rapids seen from bridge, but curds of ice still at occasional spots along bank."

As if providing a snapshot for a later gesture drawing, my jottings then focused on a figure at the side of the road, with: "... the gait of the obese ... leaning backward... umbrella swinging dangerously wide from arm dangling at a typically wide angle..."

As I got nearer to home, the antics of an Asian toddler on the bus briefly captivated me. Seeming almost half the height of his diminutive father, he was proving cumbersome in arms, and chattering happily in a foreign language, punctuated here and there by the familiar sound, "Pa-pa!" Without conjuring the image of the western Dad, the scene nevertheless pictured a father's doting attention.

On Baseline, that road with one sidewalk in Ottawa and the other in Nepean, the Ottawa side in a certain area seemed greener than the other, so my jottings described its appearance as: "... approaching 'lush' ... fertilized? ... Seedlings sprouting, or are they suckers?"

Passing by the supermarket where we usually shopped, I noted: "... short-cuts across grass to plaza and bus-stop now visible ... (mud / snow-hidden before) ... cuts off minutes of walking."

Then, looking out on an apartment building with generous lawns, I scrawled: "... gardeners' work off to early start ... what remains of brown leaves after the thaw, heaped around roots of still-bare trees on wooded plot."

New Working Environments

2001 census figures for Ontario place the unemployment rate for males slightly higher than that for females.[4]

The work experience in the public schools was not all pleasant, so I made notes when struck by positive observations.[5] My jottings on Tuesday, April 18, recorded a good day in what impressed me as a well-run school. To begin with, one of the first people I came across in the hallway was singing! It was very early, so I wasn't sure whether he was a teacher or a janitor, but I relished the pleasant sound as a herald of a good day. Singing or humming through

---

4.   Statistics Canada's Internet Site, http://www.statcan.ca/english/Pgdb/People/ Labour/labour07b.htm, August 12, 2002

5.   See also, Appendix (letter to the Graduating Class of the mission school, dated June 7, 2000)

the busyness of a day is quite the habit among some Jamaicans, but had so far been unheard here.

The principal at this school was a man, and it seemed he didn't often have supply teachers in; for he personally took the time to show me around the part of the school that I needed to know, gave me an "Occasional Teacher" badge, and the keys to the classroom where I would be supplying. The badge he explained, not only as an aid to security on the campus, but as an assurance of ready assistance from regular members of staff if necessary.

That was not the last I saw of him either. At the beginning of the day, the principal visited the classroom, introduced me to the class, and delivered not just a pep talk, but a warning to students about their conduct. He showed me the intercom unit and gave instructions for calling the office if necessary. After about an hour, he put his head briefly in at the door again to ask if all was well. It was. After registration, following the work-plan left me by the class teacher, I had sent one behaviorally challenged student off to his special program with a teacher's aide (T.A.) who came to pick him up. Then we had settled down in the atmosphere of students well trained to work quietly, encouraged by points daily awarded on the chalk-board for the tables displaying teacher-approved work habits. At recess, the principal was again on the beat, imposing his presence just briefly on the playfield.

On another April day, I had a pleasant surprise. It was an invitation from the school where I had first volunteered—to be feted at a luncheon in honor of their volunteers, as part of the volunteer appreciation plans of the OCRI[6] Volunteers in Education Program. I couldn't attend the luncheon because I was supplying that day; but later, I collected a monogrammed copy of OCRI's Thank-you publication, with my name gratifyingly recorded under the A's in the center-spread. Going to great lengths to *record* thanks was, unfortunately, not a Jamaican custom. We did, of course, *say* "Thanks," or return gifts for favors received; but in keeping with our sociologist-defined character as an "oral society," "Thank-you" cards and letters were little used, let alone publications to simply record thanks.[7]

By mid-June, my little, green logbook showed that I had worked in about ten different schools, although some school personnel didn't write the name of the school when they signed it. June 15 found me answering an unusual and desperate call—to supply in the 6th grade of a French Immersion school,

---

6.   Ottawa Centre for Research and Innovation
7.   See Appendix (letter published in *The Gleaner*, July 4, 2000).

although I couldn't speak a word of French. It was an interesting day. Students had special permission for that day to speak English—only to me, and only as necessary—while I supervised their classroom activities and interactions. The outworking of that was quite amusing, but we shared a pleasant day; they completed the work assigned by the class teacher, and nobody seemed any the worse for her one-day absence.

Occasionally, I was called in to supply in a Kindergarten class. On one such occasion, there was a teacher's aide (T.A.) in the classroom, assigned to work with two students who had special learning challenges. She worked with this class and their regular teacher every morning, and I was glad for another pair of eyes that were more familiar with this fidgety group than mine. Yet, the events of that morning defied the surveillance of all adult eyes, and proved the scariest of my supply teaching experiences.

As I got the group settled on the carpet for "circle time," and myself settled facing them, one little boy showed me that his friend had a problem. This friend had arrived at school with a small marble, which he had shown to a couple of the other boys but otherwise kept in his pocket. Then, while the children were moving about to form the circle, he had pushed the marble up into one nostril, where it was now apparently stuck.

In the minutes that followed, the T.A. took him to the office and called his home. His grandmother said she would come to get him, and he was soon off to the doctor's office. Meanwhile, I stifled my natural, habitual recourse in situations that threatened the well-being of students entrusted to me, which was to pray publicly. It seemed a grave enough threat to warrant us praying as a class for the little one endangered by the morning's mischief. But I reminded myself that this was North America, and I was not in a Christian school. So, instead, I gathered the circle into a closer huddle, and after delivering a little lecture, had them close their eyes and observe a few moments of silence, to "think" about what had just happened. In their silence, I directed the voice of my spirit heavenward, and then we resumed the scheduled activities.

I kept hoping for an offer of regular employment at the Christian school where I still occasionally supplied, but there was no staff vacancy on the horizon; so I got ready to respond to the District Board's vacancy list, which I was told is usually published in June. At the public school where I was most often called in over the next couple of months, staff morale was low, disciplinary problems were unsuccessfully dealt with, and the principal's attempts at management were more successful by her own account, than by what other eyes could see.

Nevertheless, with her encouragement, I decided to apply for employment there, since that is where I had worked most frequently. At 9:30 a.m. on June 13, the District Board posted the Vacancy List memorandum on their website, and a hard copy was circulated in the staff room of the school where I was working that day. It was nine pages in all, and stated in the preamble:

"When making recommendations to fill these positions, principals MUST give consideration to candidates in the following order:

1.) teachers seeking a transfer and part-time contract teachers who wish to increase their contract status;
2.) current occasional teachers;
3.) any other applicants.

… Teachers interested in any of the vacancies below should contact the school where the vacancy exists by phone or FAX as soon as possible to indicate their interest."

My application was faxed off as soon as I got home that afternoon. The next morning I went to supply at the school to which I had applied, and took the opportunity to ask the principal whether she had received my application. She replied that, for the two vacancies advertised, she had received over 200 faxed applications, and then the fax machine had broken down, so she wasn't quite sure whether mine had been received. I didn't need to hear any more. I recalled the unsolicited advice, bestowed earlier by one of her departing staff members, against applying for employment there for various reasons. Then, I reminded myself of Romans 8:28.[8]

New "Critters"

As we moved into our first Canadian summer, we met Ottawa's "critters" one by one, and came to respect their prior claim to the environment. The groundhogs had surfaced first, not really resembling anything Jamaican— they were too rotund—popping out of ditches and moving lazily along the verges of roads and highways. It was on the roads also, that we learnt to

---

8. "For we know that in all things God works for the good of those who love Him, who have been called according to His purpose."

recognize the infamous smell of a skunk. Though offensive, it was not quite as bad a stench as I had thought. The awful thing was that without chemical intervention, it did not go away! I heard that tomato juice could be used to wash the smell off, but thank God, I never had to try it.

The squirrels were all over our townhouse lawns, scampering up and down the trees. Always unbelievably busy, they actually seemed like little people—models of industry, but at the same time, indulging in frisky, lighthearted fun. One town-house occupant stubbornly left nuts near her door to feed them, to the chagrin of some neighbors, who thought the squirrel population certainly needed no booster. Their reputation as pesky destroyers of newly planted gardens prevented some of the green-thumbed from appreciating how "cute" they were.

Raccoons were another matter altogether. I could easily have labeled them "public menace number 1," after the warming weather eliminated the convenience of refrigerated garbage. Storing garbage in our backyard bin between collection days had been no problem at winter and spring temperatures, for it was either frozen or too chilled to attract unfavorable attention. Little did we know that raccoons were waiting in the wings to start foraging at the earliest opportunity. Like the stray dogs that abound in Jamaica, they soon made garbage disposal more challenging. Much smaller than dogs, they proved nonetheless just as brazen, inviting face to face confrontation rather than running away at the appearance of mere humans.

The locking mechanism of our garbage can cover was child's play for them. Mike and Joe used one strap, then two in various ways, to tie the cover on each night, before we finally outsmarted them. After that, we were spared the dash to the patio door to glare past our scattered garbage, into their triumphant eyes that glared right back at us. They knew they had been licked, so they didn't bother to come around any more.

A couple of months into this "new critter" learning experience, we had the most horrific lesson ever. One night, Spenser and I were awakened by alarming, swooshing, flapping sounds and air movements over our heads. We had a beautiful finished basement that we had chosen to use as our bedroom suite; and in a few seconds, Spenser realized that our airspace had somehow been invaded by two bats! For the next several minutes the war was on! I hid under the comforter till Spenser got one caught between the basement window and the external screen, and the other driven up to the main floor. Then, I made a dash up the two flights of stairs to close Deb's door and awaken Joseph. He and Mike then spent what seemed like forever, chasing and dodging the bat on the main floor, trying to get it to the front or back door, and out of the house. The critter didn't seem to get the message that flying out through a door was its safest bet, or perhaps, it just couldn't find the door. So, finally, Joe's swipe with a broom stunned it, and presumably, it awakened out on the grass. Mike got rid of the one that had been trapped in the basement window, and we concluded that they had perhaps come in via the chimney. But, in later discussions with the neighbors, we learnt there was something amiss in the roofing between townhouses, which might also have let them through.

Of course, there were bats in Jamaica, but the closest contact we had ever had with them was seeing several of their corpses scattered on the hillsides in 1988, after hurricane Gilbert had blown off most of the roofs in our district. Our ceilings had generally kept bats out of the houses, even if they lived in the roofs.

Over the next few months, we glimpsed the occasional deer as we sped past woods along the highway, but never long enough for me to get a good look. I have mentioned before, how much green space there is within Ottawa's city limits; creeks, little woods and large "green belts" are a part of the charm retained in Ottawa's development as a "city of villages."[9] Where we lived in the west end, the most westerly suburb, Kanata, was just a few minutes' drive away. After that, there was the true forest. The significance of this escaped me, till the news media reported the casual visit of a real, wild bear to the periphery of a school's playground in Kanata. Sparking some panic among the population of that area, the incident also drew comfortless comments from environmentalists, who pointed out that the bears' habitat had so recently been invaded by the new development, that they had not yet abandoned it totally.

Even in Jamaica, Mike had been the one to favor country living, always wanting wide, open spaces between his home and the neighbors', and caring very little about the lack of urban conveniences. There, our feeble objections had sometimes seemed trite, even in our own ears, compared to the benefits of living in the Blue Mountains rather than in Kingston. But here, I would not be a pushover in any move to get closer to the critters "out there" than we were at the moment.

---

9.   *The Ottawa Citizen*, November 30, 1999

Chapter 17

Summer Fruit

"For we know that in all things God works for the good of those who love Him, who have been called according to His purpose."
Romans 8:28, New International Version, the Bible.

In the months since Christmas, Ari had received her acceptance from the Canadian Montessori Academy, and we had paid most of the fees in advance, as required by their fee payment policy. We had made sure of the refund policy, and deferred the final payment, because Ari had yet to apply for a visa to study in Canada. She was now living on her own in our rural family home, and having to spend sometimes two hours traveling each way between home and work in the city. Over-zealous in her job, and physically taxed from the rigors of Jamaican public transportation, she was hard-pressed to find time for the trip to the Canadian High Commission, with its very limited hours of being open to the public. So she waited for the mid-term break in May, to schedule it.

Her delay might have been the reason for the heartache that followed; who knows? But rather than skip ahead of myself, I'll give you the blow by blow account of what happened. Ari was called in to the High Commission for the customary interview, where she presented the documents we had been warned were necessary, including those from the Academy. The interviewing officer asked her to also provide proof of our ability to finance her study period. She was told that we could fax supporting documents to the High Commission from Canada. The next day we faxed the required information, as well as photocopies of receipts from the Academy, verifying that most of the fees had already been paid.

On June 26th, Ari told us on the phone that she had been called in for a second interview at the High Commission, and from her exchange with the officer on the phone, she was sure that she would just be picking up the visa. She called because she knew we had already stretched the Academy's deadline for final payment. They had extended grace as far as possible because of the pending visa, so I went right away and submitted the final check.

Bitter Fruit

When Bell Canada's special long distance ring sounds in our house, it usually causes a quickened heartbeat. For some reason, the response to that particular ring is something akin to the response in my parents' generation to a telegram, even if we have been expecting the call. Ari didn't have email access at home or at work, so we were listening for that ring after her scheduled interview. When it came, I was alone at home. The tremor in Ari's voice made me weak at the knees. She had been denied the student's visa. She was not just tearful and despairing, but livid.

Knowing we had supplied all the documentation requested, Ari had been surprised when the officer asked her some questions she thought unreasonable; and she had replied to the best of her ability but with mounting frustration. She had been asked for evidence of "ties" such as personal property in Jamaica, or some romantic involvement. Her incredulous response had pointed out the improbability of her having amassed any personal wealth at the age of 22, working in Jamaica as a Kindergarten teacher. And no, she did not happen to have a fiancé! Knowing my daughter, I figured emotion had got the better of her, and painted the interviewer a less than subservient profile of this particular applicant.

When he delivered the verdict, "visa denied," Ari asked to be told the reason. He said that he believed she was planning not to return to Jamaica. So, here she was an hour later, calling from her Grandmother's, choking backing the sobs on the phone to me, my knees by now having let me down easy on the carpet. This was a replay of the December trauma, which had ended well; so, before long, I was speaking calming words of expectation that we could again prepare a successful appeal. I was scheduled to go to Jamaica on business anyway, and the plan had been that Ari and I would return to

Ottawa together, in time for a few days of commuting orientation before the July 11 commencement of her course. So, I would leave as quickly as possible, and help her with the tedious process of mounting an appeal.

Before I left Ottawa, we contacted the local Citizenship and Immigration department to seek their intervention, but were told that they do not interfere in such matters. During the first couple of days in Jamaica, Ari and I mustered all the new character references we could, as well as a new letter from her employers, reaffirming their approval of her study leave, and their expectation that she would return to work after the year's break. At the High Commission, we submitted these additional documents with a covering letter requesting a review of Arianne's case. We were not allowed to speak with an officer, but just given a date, July 13, on which to return. Nor could we get any apparent consideration of the fact they already had on file—that her course would begin on July 11.

In the interim, there were arrangements for the tenancy of our property and the management of the coffee farm, which needed to be pursued. One evening, I attended the Graduation and Awards ceremony of the neighboring mission school, and received a surprise gift—a beautiful plaque with a citation from the Board, thanking Mike and me for our "long, outstanding and dedicated service" to the school.

The expatriate members of staff, who had completed their two year contracts as senior teachers and acting administrators, would shortly be returning home. They were gratified by my letter, recently sent from Ottawa and published in Jamaica's main newspaper, commending them and others who serve Jamaica's institutions on a voluntary basis, or without competitive salaries. They were largely responsible for staging this very impressive function, which, along with the academic results reported, reassured the community that the standard of performance the school had established over the years would continue. The newly recruited Jamaican who would shortly assume headship was also among their distinguished guests.

In Ottawa, Mike advised the Academy of Arianne's problems, and her possible late arrival for the start of the course. In Jamaica, I encouraged her to finish packing while we waited, but she was very reluctant to get her hopes up. She was steeling herself to the prospect of a change of plan, while I was refusing to think of that eventuality. No doubt, various sermons on "faith" and its application could be woven around the thoughts and actions that occupied us at that time, but the outcome was what we both dreaded. We reported to the High Commission on July 13, were called to a window after a long wait, and handed a letter signed by the Senior Immigration Officer which stated:

"…I am not satisfied that you will adhere to the terms and conditions of a student. As a result, your application for a student authorization has been refused."

Describing here how I felt then is just too hard. Ari pursed her lips, squared her shoulders, and tried to summon the optimism of youth, which I suddenly knew I had outgrown. She would be all right, she tried to convince me over the next day and a half of heart-to-heart talks, while I rambled on about whatever I felt would be critical for her to remember as she faced the inevitable loneliness ahead. We were all agreed that she should not remain living alone so far out of the city, so she began to make arrangements to board with the mother of her best friend in town.

Sean and his bride had spent three months blissfully unencumbered, but now I urged him to keep deliberate tabs on his sister, for she wasn't one to come ringing his doorbell with her needs. At the airport on July 15, they gave up trying to stem my tears, and just kept supplying Kleenex and handkerchiefs. After we said our final goodbyes, I resorted to the rest room of the departure lounge to try and pull myself together. There, I met an old friend, the wife of a Christian cell-leader with whom we had once been associated. She said her sister was in the diplomatic service, and that she felt there must be some recourse for us. We shouldn't give up, she encouraged. That was what I needed to hear, spoken by a voice outside of my own head, in order to take heart and dry my face.

In the days that followed, Mike and I rehearsed the sequence of events that had led up to this: our deliberations, financial planning, communication, and prayers. Our inescapable conclusion was that God Himself had apparently decided that Arianne should not come to Canada at this time. He does sometimes impose hard decisions, which run contrary to our well-laid plans and earnest petitions, but serve His higher purposes and our ultimate good. Ironically, as we had grown to discover, these purposes often include answers to our more enlightened prayers—those of eternal merit with which we have under-girded our lives. So, for reasons we could only guess at, it seemed that this must be one of those times.

We secured a refund from the Academy of all but the $500 application fee, and an offer of deferred acceptance for Arianne in the following year's course. This was all we could manage at that point. Mike's new job often had him working late, and bringing home on-line work that occupied a couple more hours each evening. I had decided to leave the teaching profession till I could secure a position in a Christian school. Continued supply teaching was not appealing, because I neither enjoyed the itinerant aspect nor the unpredictability of it, and the proceeds to date were not very encouraging. For the rest of July, I pursued other kinds of job opportunities that I had identified before leaving for Jamaica.

In addition to increased income, my medium-term aims were to gain accounting qualifications and any related experience, for which I could envision much use in the future. A casual acquaintance, whom I was only prompted to call as a result of a dream, had suggested the idea of applying to certain banks, for she thought they hired trainee tellers from time to time. While following this advice, I placed eggs in every other promising basket, sending out résumé after résumé after résumé. Finally, on August 1, when the preferred job prospect with a particular bank had failed to materialize, I started a part-time job at the customer service desk of a large department store. Less than a week into this new position, the candidate to whom I had lost that other opportunity withdrew her application, and I received the very welcome offer of training and regular, part-time (10:00– 2:00, five days a week) employment as a bank teller. The department store was amenable to reducing my hours rather than letting me go, so I retained both jobs—the bank in the "morning" and the store in the evening—with an hour to grab a bite and commute between them.

Sweet Summer Fruit

In 2000, the average household in Ottawa spent almost 10% of its income after tax on recreation.[1]

The annual warming of Ottawa holds traditional delights. First, there is the Tulip Festival in May, when faithful efforts produce millions of cultured tulips that attract hordes of tourists. Visitors can take a particular route through the blooming city, often specially catered to by OC Transpo shuttles. This festival dates back half a century, and commemorates the 1945 gift of 100,000 tulip bulbs, presented by Princess Juliana of the Netherlands. This

---

1.   Statistics Canada's Internet Site, http://www.statcan.ca/english/Pgdb/People/Families/famil10c.htm, Aug. 13, 02.

was in appreciation for Canada's provision of safe haven to Holland's exiled royals in the Second World War, as well as the role of Canadian troops in liberating the Netherlands. The tulips headline a horticultural display at particular sites, lasting through the summer months.

Another summer attraction for tourists and holidaying Canadians is the Changing of the Guard, a daily military parade on Parliament Hill, dating back to a 1959 visit of Her Majesty Queen Elizabeth II, and associated with daily mounting a new Guard at the Governor General's residence. A company from the Governor General's Foot Guards (with which Chief Cousin's son used to be a trumpeter) combines with a company from another regiment and the 57-strong Band of the Ceremonial Guard, to present the daily parade. They become a bright, hot stream, in red and black uniforms relieved by white belts, that flows to the pulse created by the band, along a well-beaten course to and from Parliament Hill.

As Canada sunned itself in the summer of 2000, a personal support network of new acquaintances, neighbors and Christian friends had begun to emerge around us. Deb and Joe were the oldest and only black "kids" on the block, and much in demand from admiring teeny-boppers; the little ones wanting toys repaired or disputes settled, the pre-teens wanting a parent-trusted chaperone for movie nights, and the occasional parent wanting a baby-sitter. In addition, Joe took the first two courses toward Life Guard certification, and Deb began a working relationship with a family that needed an occasional caregiver for their disabled son. She earned a tidy sum attending him through a two-week residential summer camp, and continued afterward to provide weekend service to the family.

We had also become members of the church to which I had introduced Mike on New Year's Eve. We were getting to know people there, and with the help of the same member who had first offered us transportation, Deb and Joe were attending the mid-week youth gatherings. When Mike's schedule became more predictable, the arrangement became more of a car pool, with him usually doing the drop-off, and her, the pick-up. Once or twice, when Deb and Joe wanted to go badly enough and the car pool had fallen through, they took two buses across town.

After just two months' work, Mike's advantage from his years of experience in catering to corporate customer satisfaction was paying off more than he realized. Unknown to him, a client reported on his superior service, in response to the company's invitation for customers to identify service "heroes"—"employees and partners who have gone above and beyond the normal call of duty." Weeks later, he was on another service call to the same office, and the client was shocked when it became evident that he knew nothing of the commendation. So, she wrote to the company's headquarters in Toronto, strongly suggesting that some recognition be forthcoming for his efforts. Obviously annoyed that her recommendation had apparently been disregarded, she was also probably aware of the subtle ways in which the service of black people in a white society, or eager newcomers in a jaded workforce, is often downplayed.

Some time later, the company presented Mike with a nicely mounted letter, dated July 12, and a figurine, in recognition of his contribution to customer satisfaction, and to mark his induction into their "Heroes Hall of Fame." After a few more weeks, he was offered direct employment on staff, to replace his indirect employment as a contract worker hired through another company. All very flattering, and it did come with a benefit package, but no increase in take-home pay.

When he was comfortable enough with the routine of the job, and had brought the take-home work under control, Mike decided to try doing some sales on the side. He registered with a long-distance telephone service provider, went through a weekend orientation workshop, and began to try his hand (his mouth, really) at marketing their product. This was not a huge success, although we did have a small network of family and Jamaican friends whose long-distance phone usage made them immediate and willing candidates. The weak link lay in the company's inferior service at their call-centre, which eventually frustrated customers who tried to communicate directly with them. But Mike's start-up efforts, and the compelling company hype, held sway for some time.

Savoring the Last of Summer

By the end of August, I had made fair progress in learning the ropes of both new jobs. My middle-aged brain wasn't doing too badly at the basics of computerized banking systems, though the late evenings between the cash register and ever-ringing phone of the store's customer service desk were a greater challenge. The average customers wanting goods exchanged, or their money back, were quite polite, and even patient with the lapses of a new trainee; but there was the occasional, belligerent person, suffering less gracefully from the same end-of-the-day syndrome that I was.

Nevertheless, I was pleased with my progress on the learning curve, and still wanted to start evening courses leading to that accounting qualification, as quickly as possible. The fall term would soon be under way, and the main campus of a reputable community college was quite close to home. So, I registered for the computer course which was a pre-requisite to Accounting 1, as it involved only one 3-hour class and a homework assignment per week. One beautiful thing about summer here is that evenings are very long, bestowing daylight up to and sometimes past 9 p.m. This I found very convenient, and wondered why institutions suspended classes in August, rather than maximize benefit to (and income from) people who could not yet afford to go off to "the cottage" or other traditionally Canadian vacations.

For our part, year 2000 vacation activities consisted of entertaining Gail and Mike's Mom. Without any difficulty obtaining a Canadian visitor's visa, Gail came up from Massachusetts in the last week of July by bus, on a week's break from her on-campus summer job. She would pay her first visit to Ottawa, and then have us drive her down to Darien Lake in New York State, to meet friends headed for "Kingdom Bound," a Christian music festival there. The Changing of the Guard, the jolly buskers on pedestrian designated Sparkes Street, the Ottawa River Tour boats, museums and galleries were the local sights she took in, with Deb as most constant tour guide.

Then, on the long weekend afforded by Colonel By Day, we made our first border crossing by car to the U.S., at the Thousand Islands International Bridge. Up to this point, "Thousand Islands," in my mind, was just the name of a good salad dressing. Now, I warmed to the story of this spectacular place, where the St. Lawrence River is dotted with innumerable islands and plied by cruise boats, downstream from where Lake Ontario empties into it. Especially touching was the story of Heart Island, named for its artificially created heart shape. This was the famed, expensive, turn-of-the-century project of Mr. Boldt, owner of both the island and the equally renowned Waldorf Astoria Hotel in New York. He was building a 120-room castle on the island for his wife, when she died in 1902, and all construction was stopped.

Jamaicans and keen tourists to our own north-east coast will recall the equally touching and very similar story of Port Antonio's Folly Castle, built in the early 20th century by millionaire Dan Mitchell. It was one of the romantic stops on the leisurely honeymoon tour that Mike and I took in 1974, and when we returned with the children to see the ruins years later, they hadn't changed much.

The seven-hour drive to Darien Lake via Buffalo Airport, where we picked up Gail's friends, ended in a restful sleep-over at a small motel. We slept; the youths not as much. The next day we headed back, leaving the young music enthusiasts to enjoy the festival being staged at Six Flags amusement park. Two days later, Gail called, jubilant with the news that the "New Talent Search" (Kingdom Bound's contest for unsigned bands) had been won by her friends, the visiting Christian rock band from Jamaica, called The Few. With this, a new feather in her patriotic cap, she was heading back to campus and back to work.

Mike's mom flew from Jamaica to New Jersey late in August, and spent a week there with her adopted daughter, a U.S. resident of many years. Then, she flew on up to Ottawa at the beginning of September. She too had been granted a Canadian visitor's visa without any problems. This time, Deb took her on the double-decker tour bus, rather than the river boat, for her first bit of sight-seeing. School started that same week; so, after that, Mike dropped her off in the mornings at museums and galleries, while Joe did his bit in the evenings, taking her for walks along his favorite neighborhood trails.

The icing on my cake was getting home from work on an evening to find a dinner of traditional Jamaican cuisine—expertly prepared by the family's undisputed, champion gourmet cook—steaming and ready to be served. Then, on the weekend, Mike and I took her driving and stopped for a walk through Dowes Lake Park, where she posed for take-home pictures amongst the beautiful creations that were the second love of her life—flowers.

For the rest of September, life was very hectic.[2] I was still writing articles and selling the occasional advertisement for the monthly paper, working on this manuscript, and coordinating the smooth running of home affairs. Then, the bank requested that I take on additional hours at the beginning of October. Their hourly rate of pay was appreciably more than that of the store, so I relinquished the evening job without much regret.

Try, Try, Try Again?

After life had settled down somewhat, Mike wrote a letter to the Canadian High Commission in Jamaica, requesting some indication of whether Arianne's application for a student's visa the following year could possibly

---

2.   See Appendix (letter to Home Church brethren, of September 26, 2000, 1:07 p.m.).

stand a chance of success, given that her financial and marital status were not likely to have changed significantly by then. What were the "terms and conditions of a student" to which they had judged that Arianne would not adhere, and what would they accept as assurance that she would? Without this information, it would be foolish to repeat the application process a few months later—perhaps just an act of throwing good money, time and effort after bad.

The curt reply referred us to "Canadian Privacy legislation" that prohibited release of information from Arianne's file, and offered "regret" that the signing officer could not "be of further assistance in this matter." Back at the Citizenship and Immigration Office in Ottawa, we were told of the Live-in Caregiver Program, through which an applicant comes to Canada on contract to work in a private home for two years as a live-in caregiver, and may thereafter apply for residency. However, the catch was that the candidate should have certification as a care-giver, or a letter from an employer attesting to her work in that capacity for at least a year. The clerk who spoke with us did not think that Arianne's three years of successfully teaching and tending 2 to 4-years olds would be considered equivalent experience. Our last resort would be to start calling immigration lawyers in search of a more positive prognosis. But Ari's communications had begun to sound less distressed and more content, so we decided to just let the matter drop for a while.

Chapter 18

A Year's Worth of Lessons

"In the five years leading up to the 2001 census... the number of deaths rose primarily because Canada's population is aging. Also the number of births declined... with natural increase declining, immigration accounted for more than one-half of Canada's population growth between 1996 and 2001.[1]

My journalizing days were definitely over. The only writing I had time for over the next nine months was the tabloid column, and the slow development of this manuscript. By the tenth month, I had asked to be released from my commitment to the paper, and turned my attention toward an unimpressive cache of mismatched, loose leaves, bearing scribbled tidbits of noteworthy things that I had learnt over the months. Usually written during a break at work (but hardly any more on the bus, as my routine rides were now too short) they covered information I had not managed to glean before.

Now, here we were, in the summer of 2001, having been in Canada for almost two years. Toronto Cousin had warned that it would take about five years for us to feel at home here; and now I wondered, "Am I almost half-way there?" We didn't feel very much at home, but perhaps that's because the first half of the adjustment period was the weightier. On the other hand, we had made enough acquaintances, and renewed enough friendships in Canada's immigrant community, to have heard many tales that made our

---

1.   Statistics Canada's Internet Site, http://geodepot2.statcan.ca/Diss/Highlights/Page2/Page2_e.cfm, August 12, 2002

own challenges pale in comparison—leaving us poignantly aware of God's favor on us.

One of Chief Cousin's friends, a single woman who came here many years ago, told us of the depths of despair to which she sank sometimes as a new immigrant. Once, during a long wait at a lonely bus stop, late one winter's night, she was reduced to tearfully muttering to herself and God, "Lawd, a weh me a do ya—eena dis ya country? Mi waan' guh 'ome!"[2] Another friend related his descent into depression and suicidal contemplations, in the face of unyielding financial problems during his first couple of years here. That had reminded me of a girl I once saw wandering around Baseline (bus) Station, muttering constantly to herself in a Caribbean accent—apparently harmless, but also apparently having given up on staying in touch with the reality around her.

In contrast, our own coping mechanisms had served us fairly well so far, by the grace of God. Continuing his habit of several years, which was begun in concert with his fellow Elders at our Jamaican congregation, Mike fasted every Wednesday. But now, his prayers focused on the concerns of our recently-scattered tribe. So, we dealt with the hurdles as they popped up.

For me, the evening courses had gone very well. I had completed three of the six required for a Bookkeeping Certificate, with A and A- grades. Nature was on my side in the summer and fall; but I have to sound a "Woe!" to those new immigrants from warmer climes who attend evening classes in the winter. The sun disappears early, and whatever your mode of transportation, "It bitta out deh!"[3] Mike was happy to pick me up; so, apart from getting to work, my bussing days were largely over.

Both Mike and Chief Cousin had been on my case about getting back behind the wheel, and I had obliged (and stalled) them by taking the written test and getting the G1 license back in April 2000. But it was only when I began to find the traffic patterns predictable that I seriously considered beginning to wean myself of the buses. Then, the story of a man blind in the right eye, and yet a very confident driver, struck me when I read it in *The Ottawa Citizen*. It didn't prove that he could have done as well in Jamaica's left-hand-drive environment, as I would need to do on Canada's right-hand-drive roads with my useless left eye; but it was still an encouragement. After

2.   "Lord, what am I doing here – in this country? I want to go home!"
3.   Jamaican Creole, meaning, "It is bitterly cold and unpleasant outdoors."

all, road users here were undeniably more disciplined than those in Jamaica, which made driving safer for everyone.

So, after some preparation with a driving instructor, I took the road test and got the G2 license. By the end of the year, Deb had also taken her road test, and Joe his G1. When I examined it, I realized that the rigors of starting life over at age 45 in a new country had taken a significant toll on my self-confidence. Acquaintances at home in Jamaica, used to seeing me manoeuvre our double cab pick-up round the blind corners of the narrow mountain roads, and deftly negotiate steep, slippery, unpaved sections muddied by heavy rain, would hardly believe this new reticence. Here, even with the G2, I drove only when necessary, taking what friends called "the back-roads," and avoiding the highways for a long time.

Workplace Lingo

There was a new workplace culture to learn too. To start with, the conservatism that middle-class workers in Jamaica expect of work-place relations was not present at the bank. Everyone was expected to be on a first name basis with everyone else, including the manager. The dress code here was casual compared to that of a Jamaican bank, and I had noticed the same for teachers in many schools. With the snow and ice of winter, some niceties of fashion were shelved, unless one kept bits of clothing at the workplace. It reminded me of something an older immigrant had said to me months before: "Mi Dear, ah give dem (new immigrants) tree mont' wid dem 'igh 'eel boot de!"[4]

In the heat of summer, walking shorts were permissible work-wear for most people, from the bus driver to the bank staff to the teacher. Banter between staff members cut across all job levels in the bank, and there was an atmosphere of light conversation cultivated with customers. Even with bullet-proof glass in place at our branch, because of break-in history, there was no "distance" between staff and customers.

The paper coffee cup from a drive-through fast-food server, or the plastic coffee mug from home, was practically part of people's morning attire. Held in one's hand for sipping till one had settled at one's work station, it might there share a corner with a soda can or a juice bottle at different times of the

---

4.   Jamaican Creole, translated: "My Dear, I give new immigrants three months to give up on wearing those high heeled shoes."

day. I observed that customers didn't mind being served between sips, but my preconception of work-place manners was ingrained.

It seemed there was no unspoken code preventing the boss from getting elbow deep, at will, in taking out the garbage, getting up on a ladder to help decorate the branch for special occasions, or doing simple repairs to equipment. Nor was there anything preventing a supervisor from doing the washing-up at the lunch room sink. In fact, some with senior responsibility were eager to do what others had left undone, perhaps because of where the "buck stopped." In keeping with the culture of doing one's own housework, and to keep the "buck" climbing the competitive profit margin ladder, there was no office maid, and the minimum of janitorial work was contracted out to others who came in after office hours.

In Jamaica, remuneration to daily and weekly paid workers was called a wage, but that to monthly paid workers was a salary. There was a social difference between these classifications, and the word "pay" was more often a verb than a noun. Here, most workers across all job classifications were paid fortnightly, and everyone's earning was called their pay. Also, there was less secrecy surrounding wage details than in Jamaica. (I even heard of a private school using a fee scale based on 12% of each family's income.) Rates of pay in most classified advertisements were routinely given in hourly terms; and part-time, short-term contract, or night-shift work was more readily available and accepted than in Jamaica.

There were some differences in oral communication on the job too. I discovered, after perhaps seeming unresponsive, that giving direct commands is not the Canadian way. When the supervisor said, "You might wanna…" or "D'you wanna…" do so-and-so, she wasn't making a suggestion or asking a question. She actually meant, "Do this…," or "You should do this…," or "I want this done." Jamaican bosses were more direct. Instructions were usually clearly identifiable as such, whether prefaced or polished off with the word "please."

These differences created some confusion, especially with my breaks, as I first thought I was being offered the choice of when to take them, rather than being told, "I want you to leave *now*." (I was not accustomed to taking frequent breaks. My habit within working hours, was to work until I *needed*, for some particular reason, to knock off.) After a while on this job, it became clear what was being communicated, and I understood the supervisor's anxiety surrounding the break schedule, for she had to co-ordinate our continuous service to a steady stream of customers.

After this much time in Canada, I had come to realize that one should much less readily take a Canadian's polite words at face value than a Jamaican's. A Jamaican levelled with you in most cases, whereas Canadians seemed more prone to tell you what they thought you wanted to hear. The unfortunate result of this, for us foreigners, was that we never knew where we stood with some Canadians; so it was very difficult to talk oneself into trusting that their smile and drawing-room courtesy were actually based on goodwill. This was especially true if people's actions didn't seem to follow through. I missed the emotional security of knowing what I was dealing with, a security generously supplied by the candid responses or familiar methods of evasion common among Jamaicans.

Another departure from my Jamaican habit of being direct, seemed necessary when asking questions. I observed that questions were usually prefaced with: "I've got a question for you," or "May I ask you something?" It sounded redundant, like asking permission to ask; but it worked to secure the person's attention, and a response to your question. Also, I learnt that the word "bring" was used to mean "take" or "carry," that "good" was used instead of "well" or "fine" in answering the "How are you" question, and that "Have a good *one*" could mean good wishes for your lunch hour, your morning, afternoon, or vacation. Unfortunately, the grim warning of my older immigrant friends, about expletives used casually in the workplace, proved to be warranted. One day, I told an irate customer whose utterances had begun to go off-course, that he should be careful, because I was *allergic* to such language. Allergy is something for which Canadians have inordinate respect. They make every allowance for it, so my phrasing seemed divinely inspired that day.

Another occupant on the pedestal of Canadian attention is the animal. From following the press, it had seemed to me that the society often gave pride of place to animals over people. Now, in the workplace, this was confirmed. Fussing over pets went to such lengths that their photographs winked at you where you would have expected to see family photos. Their antics were often the talk of the day, the way I was accustomed to hearing parents and grandparents bragging about their children. Public disputes and legal battles that cast man and animal in adversarial roles were most often decided in favor of the animal; and indifference to animal welfare seemed to meet with more public outcry than indifference to human welfare.

Often incredulous about what I was reading and hearing, I recalled an incident that I hadn't thought of in years. There was a time in my early teens, when my father had been very ill, had taken early retirement, and was in the US at the invitation of American friends. He was recuperating, and gaining new knowledge and skills with which to face the future. Back in Jamaica, my mother had a lot on her plate, with a full-time job, four children, a hobby farm that was not *her* hobby, and two mongrels with the pretty phenotype bestowed by some German Shepherd genes. The older of these was my special pet, and one day he began to spin around in circles, following his tail.

By evening, when Mummy got home, the dog was obviously very sick. But at that time we lived in a part of the country where the nearest vet was a great distance away. It was already night, Mummy was bone tired, we were quite broke, and I just couldn't get her up and engaged in the task of getting this dog to a vet. I was very angry, and in spite of the home remedies that she did administer before leaving for work the next morning, the dog died.

I got over it, and after giving it some thought and observing my poor mother's continuing efforts to be all things to all her children, I retained in a mental file the picture of myself, fuming in puerile petulance over a sick animal, whose welfare I was momentarily more concerned about than that of a human being. Yes, the scripture does say, "A righteous man regardeth the life of his beast;"[5] but surely, regard for the well-being of a person takes priority.

On a lighter note, I noticed that the abuse of the word "like," which I had thought a shortcoming of North American youth, was actually a characteristic of a very wide age cohort. That was another mental change I wouldn't try to make. Fitting in just wasn't worth that much. I enjoyed using a variety of words to describe events and feelings, and wasn't about to be restricted to "… and I'm like…" so-and-so. My primary school teachers used to discourage reliance on what they called "weak words," the main offender in Jamaica at the time being the word "nice." Could those old teachers ever have imagined how narrative would suffer from abuse of the little word "like"? I mean, like… it's like…they'd be like… at a loss for words!

In the work environment of currency exchange, replete with money-borne germs, I also noticed that many people lick their fingers to turn pages and count bills. "Yuk!" A Jamaican friend, who migrated to Canada a year after we did, and had started a job in a Toronto bank, was the first beneficiary of all I had learnt the hard way. We compared notes on the phone, I helped her to understand the job culture, and clarified some misunderstandings she

---

5.   Proverbs 12:10, King James Version.

had gained from terms used in an unfamiliar way in her interview and job description.

Law and Order

Of 58,738 young offenders charged with felonies in Ontario in 1998/99, 10,978 were in Toronto. 2,498 were in Ottawa-Carleton.[6]

It occurred to me several times that the security measures of the bank where I worked, despite its retention of bullet-proof glass, would certainly not have stood the test in Jamaica.[7] The most noticeable difference was the absence of security guards. Nevertheless, in the year that I worked there, only two incidents took place that were outside the ambit of paper fraud, against which banks are constantly and expertly on their guard.

One afternoon, a cyclist left his bicycle outside the door of the bank, where bikes and motorised wheelchairs were often left. The owner, waiting his turn in the "line-up," luckily glanced toward the door at the precise moment that a nimble youth hopped onto his bicycle and took off. He let out a yell and gave chase, followed a few steps by the bank manager, who happened to have been circulating among customers at the time. Someone got on a cellphone to the police while the owner continued the chase, and before long the hapless thief was forced to relinquish his prize.

The other incident was more serious, more successful, and more of a bank-specific robbery. Because I was not full-time, I arrived at work after the incident, to find police milling about, and my entry barred till I was identified to them. Once inside, I heard accounts of what had happened, and was struck by two thoughts. Firstly, the robbers had successfully executed their plan, with staff present but before the bank was opened to the public, without a firearm or other weapon, and apparently facilitated only by a security breach in the design of the building.

Secondly, the events of the pre-dawn hours at home flashed back. I had been awakened very early and very suddenly by a single-sentence "dream." A voice had said to me, "A young man is going to die today." This kind of

---

6. Ontario Ministry of the Attorney General Internet Site, http://www.attorneygeneral.jus.gov.on.ca/html/CAD/stats98-99/tab08p02.pdf, August 13, 2002

7. See "Preface to the Second |Edition"

thing had happened often enough that I knew how to respond. In the first place, young men die every day, so this obviously concerned one who was somehow connected to us. Also, what I had experienced was like overhearing a diabolical plan, not a prediction of its certain fulfilment. Nothing was set in stone till God had finished having His say. So, I awakened Mike, told him about it, and we prayed together for the life of this unidentified young man.

Now, from the accounts of the robbery, it seemed that the service manager was that young man whose life had been endangered. The two robbers had "roughed him up," and threatened to bludgeon him with an implement held to his head, to secure his speedier compliance with their demands. As he did his best to control shaking fingers fumbling with keys, the robbers had become increasingly agitated and really seemed about to do him in, as if he were deliberately postponing their access to cash. From all accounts, and from the extent of his emotional trauma which became obvious over the next few days, he could have passed out without any help from their improvised weapon.

Accustomed to the hardiness and bravery of Jamaicans, I often found the Canadian psyche to be timid. In schools, it never ceased to amaze me how easily scared and offended the children were. They seemed emotionally very fragile, and not bolstered by any encouragement toward valour. They imagined themselves to be much frailer than the masterpieces of God's creation could possibly be.

The good side of this social psyche was gentleness, courtesy, compassion for the weak, and basic honesty in financial matters. These qualities combined to play out scenes on the other side of my bullet-proof glass, which, it seemed to me, would be wonderful if this were indeed heaven, but were scary since it obviously was not. There were, for example, sweet little old ladies who came in habitually, at predictable times, to conduct business and leave the bank with cash. Some of them couldn't see a fly if it perched on their noses. They had no way of personally verifying how much cash I had given them, and certainly not much hope of guarding it, if targeted by a thief. I had to stretch my fingers around the bottom of the glass sometimes, to help them identify the pen provided, and the delimitation of the paper on which they were to sign.

I admired this society that was so accustomed to law and order that people seemed to take beneficence for granted. Although I thanked God every day for the respite from having to worry about crime and safety, I became concerned for Canada. Several times I thought of writing a letter to the police, warning them that the society seemed wide open to be taken advantage of, by those people of criminal intent who had been socialised elsewhere. I never did write it, because I wasn't sure how it would be received—by them, or anyone else who became privy to it, and who like myself, had indeed come from elsewhere. So, why am I writing this now? Your guess is as good as mine—perhaps I just hate leaving truths out of a true story.

On the Home Front

Joseph became a super-hero to some of our neighbors one day, just by reacting to an incursion with his typical alacrity. Our neighbor's kids had lost a bicycle recently to thieves, who had simply removed the unsecured bike from their backyard. Having already witnessed the Canadian garage sales, I really wondered about the motivation for stealing a bike, when they were given away at such bargain prices by spring-cleaning householders. But this was a new, top-of-the-line model, and the neighbor had made some efforts to trace it. He had seen some strange boys loitering near his backyard before the bike disappeared, but could not find any trace of them.

On the following Saturday, Joe was relaxing before the T.V. in a comfy chair by our back door. Most of the adjacent wall was glass, and suddenly, a projectile hit the glass. In a split second, Joe saw that it was a stick, and glimpsed two heads darting away behind our five foot high garden fence. He was already through the door, calling out to them, but not waiting around for their obviously unlikely return. In a deft, practised movement, he vaulted over the far corner of the fence, ignoring the gate at the other end, to follow as closely as possible on their heels.

There were three townhouses east of us in our row, and by the time Joe turned the corner around the end unit, he had caught up with the two runners. He emerged at the front with both arms extended, holding each boy by his shirt. They were at most about 13 years old, and really scared. Mike, Deb, and the neighbor who had lost the bike, had by then gone to meet Joe and his detainees on the path. Although we had forgotten about the bicycle incident, the neighbor immediately suspected a connection, so he and Mike began to question the boys about it. Finally they admitted knowledge of the bike, saying that they knew who had stolen it, and that it was in an underground garage which served some apartments nearby.

The boys agreed to lead the way, but when they arrived, there was no bike and they could offer no explanation. Our neighbor decided not to take it any further; so, after he and Mike had warned them sternly, they took a parting glance at Joe's frame and were off. We never saw them again.

Behind closed doors, I issued my own warning to the new community hero. "Yu cyaan grab up white people like dat! Min' yu get yuself in trouble!"[8] This wasn't his mountain home, we reminded him, where his keen surveillance of family property, even as a small boy, had led to his loud confrontation of adult trespassers after our mangoes. The praedial thieves, thus rebuked, had only laughed admiringly at the audacity of this diminutive sentinel; but had he then possessed this frame to match the spirit, they might have been less amused.

We had been here long enough to realize that many black teenage boys become unsuspecting targets of unwarranted accusation, especially in altercations involving white people. Sometime, it seemed to lead to arrest without due investigation, as they seemed to be presumed guilty by virtue of their physical characteristics. My liberating optimism about the attitudes toward black people in this society had long been replaced by cautious, tiptoeing self-restraint. I had come to accept the fact that to many Canadians, we were not created equal.

On the other hand, we had been told that some white people can hardly tell us Blacks apart, and now that seemed plausible, for I had discovered that it worked both ways. Without striking hair color or other identifying marks, I often could not assign an identity to some new white acquaintance whom I was supposed to recognize. So, we also continued to warn Joseph that the Biblical injunction about avoiding the very appearance of evil[9], now had new ramifications.

He would especially have to avoid those external characteristics associated with the kind of black youth culture that attracted unwanted attention from the establishment. I think we became a bit paranoid, wanting him off the pedestrian beat earlier at night than his social life prescribed; expecting him not to take pride in the fashions and demeanor that the youth culture generally thought "cool," and trying, without the obvious means of processed hair and bleached skin, to have him groomed to seem less different from the white population. After all, we rationalized, he was here to get a tertiary education and the opportunity for better life choices; not to be picked up by some police patrol in a case of mistaken identity, while innocently bopping

---

8.   "You can't grab hold of white people like that, lest it gets you into trouble."

9.   1 Thessalonians 5:22, the Bible, King James Version

along from the bus stop around midnight with a toque or ski mask pulled down over his freezing face. Thank God, after a while the paranoia wore off.

Before our first year of regular employment was over, Mike and I were comparing notes and recalling something that a Canadian, resident in Jamaica, had told us. This lady was more Canadian than many who trace their citizenship generations back. She was a native Canadian, of mixed ancestry that included the First Nations, whose land the Europeans began to appropriate four centuries ago. (We had learnt that the modern, politically correct terms are: First Nations, rather than "Indians," and Inuit (singular "Inuk") rather than "Eskimo.")

This Canadian had warned us that employers here will try to get as much unpaid service out of employees as possible. In her own words, "They don't like to pay you." We gradually understood what she meant. People would offer you employment for X number of hours, but expect you to report to the work place significantly earlier, and be still available to them significantly later than the contractual hours. And we are not talking executive positions here. This applied more at the bottom than at the top, and working students were often the victims. The simple salve would have been to make it worth the while of the employee, who probably needed to make up the hours elsewhere to supplement a salary that was not "top dollar." But the predisposition of employers to be cheap seemed too overpowering for such rational thought.[10]

---

10.   For other events of the period summer 2000 to summer 2001, see Appendix, letters dated September 26, 2000 to May 4, 2001.

Chapter 19

"Whatsoever Things are Lovely...

... whatsoever things are of good report; if there be any virtue, and if there be any praise, think on these things." Philippians 4:8, King James Version, the Bible.

Now, in the summer of 2002, I am completing this diary, expecting that by the end of the current week, all I wanted to share will have been included for your benefit, amusement, and the glory of God. A lot has changed for the better over the past year. Mike secured a job that was more suited to his expertise, with the appropriate remuneration. My prayer for employment once again in a Christian organization was answered, and I returned to Christian Education, this time in Ottawa. But not before I had the opportunity to return to Jamaica for a month between jobs, to help the mission school through a difficult time.[1]

Deb has completed high school, and also her first year of university, with an impressive résumé of skills, accomplishments, Canadian work experience, and Canadian references. Apart from having worked in childcare programs of the YMCA, she had also worked briefly as the receptionist in a real estate office. She had made the soccer team in grade 12, and in grade 13 had represented her school on Ottawa's Community Council for Ethno-cultural Equity. Before graduating, she had also been certified in CPR[2] and First Aid; but the demands of her first year, university nursing course had precluded all extracurricular activities except the church-related ones.

---

1. See Appendix, letter of September 20, 2001, 4 a.m.
2. Cardiopulmonary resuscitation

Joe enjoyed his grade 12 co-op placement, assisting an art teacher in a high school, where he also left his stamp by painting them a mural. In addition, he gained great confidence and sales experience, working a part-time job in a store. There, he even survived a subtle attempt to frame him in an inside job burglary, when an acquaintance of the manager had dipped into the kitty while Joe was signed on at the cash register. Later, he dropped the part-time job to concentrate on pursuing a competitive average in his grade 13 OAC's. I had also put the company's honor to the test, and emailed them a letter of complaint after Joe had waited several months to receive his final paycheck, following his resignation. They passed the test, sending an apologetic email in response, as well as his check; and proving on behalf of Canada that one has recourse here for abuses which, in Jamaica, would probably never be acknowledged. On the personal side, Joe's art had continued to flourish, contributing to our home décor, art-to-order for friends, and workshop activities for the church youth group. And now, he too was all set to enter university.

As a backdrop to all of that, I had deferred completion of the bookkeeping courses, and we had moved to the other end of the city. There, Deb and Joe's social life prospered with the accessibility of many Christian peers whom they had met at church. Teaching full time, I had shelved this manuscript once more, till the summer holidays could allow its completion. Meanwhile, I realized that the differences between "the Queen's English," American, and Canadian usage involved not only nuances of spelling and colloquialisms, but also grammar. For example, the past perfect tense seemed under-utilised; colons, semi-colons and inverted commas were used differently, and a comma was permissible before the word "and." It has been amusing trying to be consistent throughout this manuscript, despite my changing applications, especially of punctuation.

Now, it's time to focus on some of the pleasures of Canadian residency which have not yet been covered. Those blessings that come readily to mind are OHIP[3], returns to taxpayers, and provision for students. Of course, as in many aspects of life everywhere, the good is so often entwined with the bad and the ugly, that mention of the clouds between the silver linings is inevitable.

We found OHIP health coverage a welcome provision, although in the first year we only used it once for my regular eye test, and twice for Deb's

---

3.   Ontario Health Insurance Plan

surprise development of joint pains in her fingers. It was wonderful not to be charged for medical or optical visits, or diagnostic procedures. The following winter, Deb slipped on ice and damaged her ankle, and Joe developed pneumonia. Between January, with Joe's speedy recovery, and June, with Deb's more protracted case, we learnt more about OHIP coverage and the limitations of the health care system.

Conclusions? Going to the doctor in Ontario was easy enough to tempt those predisposed to hypochondria; but in dealing with a clinic, it seemed that getting satisfactory treatment (leading you back to healthy independence of the clinic) was not always easy. Perhaps we were just with a badly run clinic, because, starting in January, we were sent on several laps of an amazing run-around between labs, a hospital and the clinic, without any promise of a necessary referral to the appropriate specialist before July. The government paid health service providers each time you darkened their doors, so why not keep you coming? You would have to smarten up, perhaps with help from friends, and find a good family doctor who would take a genuine interest in patients achieving and maintaining good health.

Finding a family doctor was not just a matter of making a first appointment, either. Ontario was short of licensed medical practitioners, (to differentiate from foreign-trained doctors working in other fields because of difficulty becoming licensed). Many doctors in practice considered themselves overworked, so there was some difficulty in 2002 to find Ottawa doctors who were accepting new patients. When you located one who was, the next consideration was, would he / she accept *you* as a patient? Without disclosing what the criteria for acceptance could be, some medical receptionists gave the discouraging impression that the doctor would use your first visit more to decide whether you were acceptable as a patient, than to begin addressing your health needs.

Of course, we too had to be careful in choosing family doctors. There would be obvious comfort in having one with a Caribbean background, or one having demonstrable experience with black patients. We had discovered by now that certain health care practices in Jamaica cause problems for Jamaicans in North America, when dealing with doctors who don't understand the implications. For example, the TB inoculations and boosters, given routinely to Jamaican infants and youth, often caused a reaction to the TB skin test that indicated high resistance, but was taken instead to indicate possible infection. Even when x-rays showed no sign of infection, doctors often prescribed months of antibiotic treatment, with varying side effects.

Another concern, I had heard, was over the finding of veins to work with. Medical staff only accustomed to seeing veins plainly through white skin (the story went) often went through a bit of trial and error before locating ours. I never paid any attention to this tale till I had an insurance physical, and for the first time in life, ended up with such a wounded arm from the blood test, that the swelling took weeks to subside. Of course, there could have been other reasons for that, but it made me wonder… And if I had thought of scenarios where pallor or other skin color changes might aid the medics' assessment of one's condition, I could have wondered more.

Huge Silver Linings

We did, eventually, find two family doctors we were happy with—one for the girls and one for the boys. But even before that, we had to concede that had we remained in Jamaica, Mike would probably have been five months in his grave at the time of this writing. After two years of not having demanded more of OHIP than an eye test, he suddenly became very ill with a life-threatening condition. Being taken to a hospital emergency facility for the first time in his life was no fun, especially with the painfully slow process that faced us there.

A sign on the wall literally warned patients to prepare for a four hour wait, though we later gathered that one could probably receive quicker attention if it were not a weekend, if one had called 911 for ambulance service instead of insisting on being driven to the hospital by one's wife, and if one could somehow convince the staff of impending demise. In the waiting room there were only double and single seats with arm-rests separating them. There was nowhere to lie down, recline or stretch out. If you were weak you could get a wheelchair, but if you just had the kind of pain exacerbated by not being able to lie down, this was the wrong place to be.

Not until a black Canadian friend pointed out none too patiently to the reception staff that Mike was actually turning grey, did they give credence to the extent of his pain, and the urgency of his need for at least a place to lie down. By the grace of God, after the third excruciating visit to the emergency room over a two week period, the "right" young resident made a referral to the "right" consultant, and Mike was hospitalized. With the typical Jamaican ability to "tek bad tings mek joke,"[4] we noted and laughed about the fact that we had been taken full circle, back to the first diagnosis humbly suggested

---

4.   Jamaican Creole meaning, "Make a joke out of something unpleasant."

on the very first night by the female medical student who had first examined Mike.

When you're in, though, your troubles are probably over if it's something they can fix. In short order, Mike had the first surgical procedure required, and was sent home after a couple of days. The second procedure, tentatively scheduled for two to three weeks later because of the waiting list, was actually performed after five days, as the specialist deemed his case urgent enough to warrant a reshuffling of the list. The third and final procedure was done several weeks later, when his condition had suitably improved. And the bottom line is, if he had been in Jamaica when this episode happened, he might have died. My only sister died in 1991 from the same organ failure that had threatened Mike, though hers was secondary to a different underlying condition. When we spoke with medical doctors at home about the procedures Mike had needed, they said that models of the necessary equipment were there now, but they were out of use for some undetermined reason.

Another huge silver lining to the discomforts of being relative newcomers to Canada was the government's willingness to return some tax dollars to you, in cash. In 2000, doing tax returns for our few months of residency had been tedious and brought little return. But in 2001, we had a better understanding of the system. Though the preparation of the tax return submission was still a chore, once it was submitted, dealing with CCRA (Canada Customs and Revenue Agency) was downright pleasurable. Our tax return checks that year were enough to finance advance airline bookings for a well-needed Christmas trip to Jamaica. The next time around, we found that the returns could very affordably be done through a professional, or over the Internet.

In Jamaica, it had seemed at times that the relevant bureaucracy had a secret aim of making it as difficult as possible for people to pay taxes. I recall the frustrating hours that Mike spent as a small business entrepreneur, trying to track and divest himself of the government's (then newly imposed) GCT (General Consumption Tax). The standing in line and rushing around to different departments that I had to do, to remit taxes on behalf of the mission school, brought no pleasant memories, except the monthly satisfaction of having persevered to get them paid.

All of that a world away, Canadian tax dollars had even been returned unsolicited to taxpayers below a certain income level, as the government's contribution to their heating bills in the harsh winter of 2000– 2001. I found that a very pleasant surprise, though it brought mixed reactions in the press and over the airways, because some people could think of better ways for government surplus to be spent; and because it had been distributed more widely than seemed necessary to them.

Educational Opportunities

However, it was opportunities for students that had brought us to Canada in the first place, and in this regard we found all we had hoped for. In Jamaica, Sean had applied for a student's loan to complete his degree without burdening us unfairly, in consideration of his four younger siblings. It was refused, on the grounds that the Students' Loan Bureau judged us able to support his studies. But here, when Deb had secured an offer of admission and applied for an OSAP (Ontario Student Assistance Program) loan, both the process and the response were just the opposite.

The information requested on the application form covered parent income (as recorded on tax returns), bursaries or other income the student expected to receive during the study period, and the student's plan for accommodation. However, the size of the loan being applied for was not asked, and we gathered that OSAP would determine its grant based on a comparison with the university's estimate of expenses for students in the particular program. Deb did her own calculations, offsetting the costs as given in the prospectus against her expected income, and taking into consideration the fact that she would be living at home. Her estimate, thus reached, fell significantly short of the funds subsequently made available by OSAP, perhaps in consideration of their better informed and more generous estimate of her needs. (We later found that Deb's funding would not be granted when our combined salaries exceeded some undisclosed threshold, as long as she was living at home; but that she could still apply successfully if she were not.) Furthermore, some commercial banks offered easily accessible student loans, which made good business sense. By helping young professionals-to-be, they were courting clients for life.

Some universities made an appreciable effort to encourage *all* those interested in the pursuit of higher knowledge and specific skills. I discovered that an applicant who had failed to gain admission because of low final grades at the end of a promising high school record, might actually receive an *invitation* from the university to enrol in special programs geared toward overcoming obstacles to performance, with guaranteed matriculation on satisfactory completion. Of course, not all universities took this approach, but what a wonderful safeguard this was, against wasting years of potential productivity.

In the lower echelons of North American education, children learn many skills which Jamaican youth are expected to imbibe informally through the experiences of life. As we know, especially in countries where poverty determines many life experiences, this does not produce graduates equally equipped even in basic terms. I look forward to the day when Jamaican elementary curricula will include more practical coaching that predisposes youth to early success in personal financial management, personal health management, and even road safety. Look, for example, at the following topics in Grade 7 / 8 Math: (adapted from *Pre-Algebra Basic Mathematics II*, second edition, A Beka Book Publications, USA).

> *Income: salary, hourly, piecework, commission, deductions...*
> *Taxes: property and sales...*
> *Checking Account: writing checks, deposit slips, keeping the check book balanced, reconciling monthly statements...*
> *Borrowing Money: simple interest formula, installment buying...*
> *Investments: savings accounts, compound interest formula, buying stocks and bonds...*
> *Insurance: life, health, fire, automobile...*

Even in a society where daily transactions are still very cash based, and some rural folk still stash money at home rather than using a bank, Jamaica needs to offer education which can propel arising generations towards a more prosperous future. One reason the rich keep getting richer and the poor poorer, is that the rich learn how to manage money, whereas the poor know best how to consume it. Besides, receiving instruction in school is a more efficient route to learning than trial and error in later life.

Here is an incident that gives the simplest possible example of a different kind of skill, the acquisition of which is taken for granted in Jamaica (among those for whom it is deemed necessary), sometimes with fatal results.

One day, early in my Canadian sojourn, an energetic little group passed by as I waited at the bus stop. At first I thought it might be a family; but later, I realized it might have been a caregiver and her little charges. At any rate, they were headed in the direction of a nearby day care facility. They had emerged from an intersecting avenue, five bouncing bundles of energy, helmeted and covered from head to fingertips to toes in brightly colored, warm clothing. Three on bicycles were leading the way, followed by two toddlers trying valiantly to keep up on foot, and a brave young lady pushing a large, twin-sized stroller.

Led by the little riders, they all kept to the narrow strip of paved sidewalk between the verges and lawns. Suddenly the toddlers started running, perhaps to catch up with the bikers, but the "caregiver" called out to them and they stopped immediately. The bikers raced on till they got to the next intersection, where they too stopped and waited for the others to catch up. I had wondered then at the obedience, competence and control that these tiny tots displayed in their application of road safety rules. Only in 2002 did I discover that these skills are sometimes taught to pre-school and school-age children, in workshops sponsored by insurance companies and other interested parties.

Final Gleanings

In two and a half years in Canada I have learnt a lot. One realization that has slowly dawned on me is that many immigrants, from all over the world, have a hard time settling here. Our acquaintances in Ontario now include Africans, Italians, refugees from Europe's war ravished countries, people from the Philippines, the Middle East, and other Caribbean countries. Some of us speak freely amongst ourselves of employment woes, and the role played by color, accent, fluency with English and knowledge of French. Some breadwinners have settled their families in one place and gone alone to wherever the work is; while some families have tried settling in other provinces such as neighboring Quebec, but returned eventually to Ontario. Statistics Canada's Census 2001 analysis included this note on Quebec:

> *"Montreal (Quebec) did not have as many immigrants as Toronto or Vancouver. They showed a rate of 7 a year for every 1000 people (the national average) compared to 19 for Toronto and 18 for Vancouver. Montreal (and surrounding areas) account for 52% of Quebec's population and 12% of Canada's. The rest of Quebec outside of Montreal experienced, on average, a slight decline in population."*[5]

---

5.   http://geodepot2.statcan.ca/Discuss/Highlights/Page9/Page9b_e.cfm

Our church fellowship included people of over 30 nationalities, and ever so often the senior pastor would have representatives of different countries come to the altar to stand in proxy, while the rest of the congregation interceded for their homelands. That was as immense a blessing for souls like mine, as I'm certain it was for the countries we targeted in prayer.

The ways of many Canadians are still discomfiting for us, but we have found a somewhat kindred spirit among Newfoundlanders, "Newfies" to their mainland compatriots. Newfoundland is an island of Atlantic Canada, which, together with Labrador on the mainland, joined the confederation only in 1949. It remained the youngest of the provinces and territories till 1999, when Nunavut, home to the majority of Canada's Inuit, and extending from Hudson's Bay almost to the North Pole, was granted similar status.

The first social contact I had with a Newfoundlander was at a bus stop during my initial job search period. It was in an unfamiliar part of downtown Ottawa, and I asked directions of an older man who was also waiting at the bus stop. He answered in a very thick accent, which was the first hint that he was not from Ottawa. So, I asked him where he was from, and began to hear about Newfoundland. He was very friendly and talkative, and soon asked where I was from. He said he knew a couple of Jamaicans, who were his neighbors in an apartment building downtown. Then came the sad tale of one of them, a young woman who seemed to have had no relatives or friends in Ottawa—perhaps a newcomer. He had never exchanged more than a cordial greeting with her, but had observed her going and coming regularly in the building. Then, one day, he noticed that she hadn't been seen for a while. Shortly afterwards, she was found dead in her apartment, apparently from natural causes—being very ill and all alone.

This was told in the style of a mariner's tall tale—sensational and without euphemism—and we commiserated over the fate of the poor girl. Later, I had met others from Newfoundland, and noticed their candid, yet open and friendly manner—a balmy breeze that warmed the heart, even in chilly Ottawa. By and by, Mike and I heard about the historical links between Jamaica and Newfoundland, forged through the rum-for-salt fish trade. "Screech," I learnt, was the Newfoundland label of what was widely recognized as a Jamaican rum. Salt fish, on the other hand, was historically such a staple of the Jamaican diet that it became part of our national dish, "Ackee and Saltfish."

I Miss...

I miss the colors of the Caribbean, and have resolved that the pressure to absorb the blandness of Canadian tones is not going to get to me. Why should one wear shades and patterns dictated by traditional interpretation of the weather: white and light colors only in summer, splashy colors almost never, dark colors most of the time, monochrome suits without even the relief of a cheerful inner blouse? These are the expectations that led a Jamaican friend of ours, living for several years in Toronto, to have declared quite early in her office career there, "I am a tropical bird!" She had no intention of assuming any other plumage.

I also miss the measure of privacy we have forfeited, by having our particulars automatically listed with millions of others in the First World's network of accessibility. It was a shock the first time I realized how easy it was for any organization to secure my name, address and telephone number. Jen used to say that this government knows more about us than we know about ourselves, and that is alarming enough; but what of those pesky telemarketers? These are people who (in trying to earn their bread, I must remember) invade your off hours with sales pitches, "special offers," flattery and promises, via your telephone. One service the phone company has never called to offer us is a way of screening out all these calls. They probably won't devise that, for their telemarketers are not the least annoying. Mike actually likes to hear what all these people have to say, so I know we won't miss anything important even if I keep tuning them out.

Junk mail is another unwelcome spice of this new life. It took me a while to figure out how we got onto some organizations' mailing lists, but I still haven't figured out how to get off. In one case, I wrote to the organization, stating plainly that I did not wish to receive any more mail from them, and that was two years ago. It's still coming! (In all fairness, this is an international organization and not Canadian based.) Flyers, free community papers, and more promotional coupons than anyone could possibly use, are at your front door each day to be added to your household recycling.

Another kind of junk mail is the kind of promotion intended to get you more and more into debt. Coming from a society where credit cards were a relatively new feature, and "buy-now, start-paying-later" deals did not exist, I saw a serpent's head every time some unsolicited offer of credit arrived on our doorstep. It took very little imagination to see how easy it would be to end up with more debt than one could service. But, thank God, He had long ago convinced us of the diabolical origin of debt-promoting schemes.

The most striking bit of junk mail I have received here, however, was not from an organization. It was a letter from a man in the Bronx, New York. This person, whom I don't know, wrote to me before Mike had joined us in Canada, saying that he was 43 years old and seeking my "companionship in love and friendship." After describing himself and his needs, he offered to help me with my kids, and asked me to send him a photo. I kept the letter as Exhibit Number 1, in case I should ever need to prove that this really happened.

"I Am (or am not) Canadian"

Canadians are very bristly about their relationship with the US, and anxious that others should recognize them as distinct from "Americans." This promotion of a Canadian identity, satirized in the beer commercial, "I am Canadian!" is often delivered with humor. An email circulated where I worked in November, 2001, pointed up the following trivia of Canadian-American comparison: Canadians refer to chocolate bars rather than candy bars, pop rather than soda, highways rather than freeways, grade 12 rather than the 12th grade, "pike" the fish rather than "pike" the part of a freeway. It poked fun at Canadian pacifism, by which some regard Cuba merely as a cheap tourist destination that offers good cigars and spares one the American presence. It also derided Canadians' adaptations to their harsh climate, by mentioning the height of their front doors from the ground, their reliance on the "toque"—an unfamiliar name in American fashion, and the tyranny of winter over Canadian life and business. Of course, Canadians' obsession with hockey, and their little interjection, "eh," did not escape mention.

Here are a few of my own "signs you may really be in Canada" (rather than in Jamaica):

- There are a surprising number of cars on the road that show signs of rust, which your tour guide says is caused by salt on the roads in winter.

- Intonation among the locals goes up at the end of most phrases, not just at the end of questions.

- You see a sign outside a lawyer's office that reads "No Solicitors."

- You see a shingle outside another office identifying the firm as "Richer and Richer—Attorneys." It makes no sense till you hear the French pronunciation.

- You observe a man dressed in a suit as if for work, walking a small dog on a leash downtown. He pauses behind the dog, picks up its excrement with a plastic-bag-gloved hand, and heads into a high-rise building, dropping the bag into a bin at the door.

- You see your neighbors for less than half the year (only when it's warm), although you share a wall and a frontage of unfenced driveways with them.

- You hear tales of people storing food in containers beneath the snow, on their lawns, when their refrigerator was filled to capacity.

In the less chilly months:

- You see an adult roller-blade to the steps of an office building, sit on the steps, change into her indoor shoes, and enter for work.

- Students roller-blading along the sidewalk pass your car at the traffic lights, hands swinging free, with their backpacks buckled securely in place, on their way to school.

- You recognize a female Member of Parliament next to you at a traffic light downtown, unescorted, helmeted, astride a Harley Davidson, on her way to work.

- You notice that the military still has significant resources devoted to playing music and providing public entertainment.

- You notice that enclosed garages are used more for storage than for parking, and are often left open, with their contents on display at the front of the house.

- On a highway in the city, you are overtaken by a biker, followed by a group of others, both male and female. They are dressed in black leather to their toes and fingertips, some towing luggage attachments and some with pillion riders. Finally, the whole entourage is disappearing fast, way ahead of you on the highway.

- On the same highway, a relatively small car is ahead of you with a bicycle rack on top. No less than three bicycles are standing upright above the car, doubtless strapped securely to the rack; but nevertheless you waste no time in getting out from behind them.

Finally...

In closing, it is important to note some welcome updates on Jamaican situations that I have written about. For example, the telephone service monopoly has been replaced by a thriving competition involving new companies, bringing affordable and better service to remote areas. There have been improvements in Kingston's public transportation system, and the roads in many parts of the island. Also, there is now a weekly newspaper called *LOVE Herald*, devoted to religious expression.

Christians among the Jamaican Diaspora need to keep watching and praying for their homeland, not allowing the sweetness of material blessing abroad to render them forgetful. Rather, using their new access to resources, and the advantage of greater objectivity, they should resolve to become channels of blessing, yielding themselves to the Almighty as offshore instruments which He can use in various ways to bring change.

There is only one thing left to tell you, and I saved it for the last because it's unfinished business. It's about Arianne. We are still regretting that we left her in Jamaica, for she still has not been allowed to even visit us since we have all been here. Last summer, she applied once more for a visitor's visa and was denied. As we look forward to eligibility for Canadian citizenship, I am haunted by the title of the movie, *Not Without My Daughter*. But since we are taking various steps in an effort to have her join us here, I'll borrow the phrasing of another Hollywood character, Forrest Gump, who often declared, "That's all I have to say about that."

Closure is something we all treasure; even in reading a story like this. But life often postpones closure; at least till important issues are settled. If this were fiction, I could, perhaps, pick an ending out of a hat. But it's not, it's life. If you've read this far, it means you appreciate the difference, and can face reality squarely with me. My reality is one shared by many who migrate from troubled lands to safer, greener pastures. Although we value the First World's improved standard of living, the applications of technology, the relative efficiency of bureaucracy and law enforcement, we still nurse throbbing soul-ties to our homelands.

Immigration from Third World to First World countries will continue, due to the survival instincts that have preserved the human race to this point. However, many who apply to immigrate do not realize how absolutely stressful it can be to survive the changing of worlds. For some in the Caribbean, Canada seems the country of opportunity for a better life, and Canada continues to invite them here. Many applicants don't know that although the politicians and social scientists agree that the country desperately needs immigrants, this realization has not filtered down to the average Canadian, let alone the average Canadian employer. Therefore, they are not prepared for the demoralizing experiences they may encounter, trying to start life over as immigrants in Canada.

Although desperate times call for desperate measures, applicants should try to avoid leaving dependent relatives behind, because the Canadian definitions of "family" and "dependent," are different from ours, and the immigration bureaucracy here can seem totally heartless. This can leave a family torn in unforeseen ways, and sour even an otherwise successful naturalization process. I daresay, Canada loses many man-hours of initiative, service, and creative entrepreneurship, from the strain put on immigrant families who are denied reunification.

If, because desperate times do call for desperate measures, applicants do have to go through an immigration process that is less than perfect, there is one foolproof gem of advice I can offer: go with God! The whole earth is His. There is nowhere that He can be stopped at the border, and no diplomacy by which He is bound. His was the only say-so on which I left Jamaica, and His are the personal promises in which I trust: that eventually, our family members will once more have free access to each other; there will be no more sorrow attached to our having become Jamaican immigrants in Canada; rather, there will be a facility of movement and enterprise, which will make me a brand new channel of blessing connecting Jamaica and Canada.

Appendix

"Dear Jamaica..."

Excerpts from my letters to Jamaicans, written 1999 to 2001, unedited except for: context inserted, some names substituted with descriptive titles, some details deleted to protect the privacy of other people or organisations, and to avoid unnecessary repetition between letters and previous chapters.

September 27, 1999, 9:33 a.m.

Email to: Home Church Fellowship
Hi All,

...I sent Mike a fat envelope of all Church # 2's handouts that I managed to get second copies of, and I'll get the others next week; but I'll just describe the setting to you. It was wonderful—the only Home Church features missing were our particular vigour, the P.A. volume (my eardrums will rest) and the dancing—next time I'll get a back seat so I can do my own thing. It may catch on. I intended to enquire about tapes of the meetings, because I wanted Mike to sample the 'word', although there is a statement of doctrine in the package I sent him...

...Isn't God good? He is restoring all I lost in terms of fellowship opportunities, living at Mountain Village! And doing it in one sweeping move! Deb has a heavy course load this semester, but Joe's is fairly light; so he, and to a lesser extent she, can also take in the mid-week activities...

...There is a particular, familiar cloud I have been aiming for in (personal) prayer, but I won't fool myself, or pretend to you that I'm even at the place with God where I was in May. There's a threshold I have never managed to

cross without fasting, and I'm going to go on a one-meal-a-day plan for this week. The problem is that Chief Cousin and Claire will worry…
Love,
Evangeline

September 27, 1999, 12:25 a.m.

Email to: Home Church affiliates in the US and UK
Hi, All Ye Scattered Abroad,

I hope this letter finds you in the joy of the Lord, enjoying prosperity of soul, body and pocket. You may have heard that we have moved—but not from me, so here goes. I have just had the time to put hands to keyboard; the last few months have been really something. I thank God for the prayers and support that brethren like you have continued to provide for me, our family and the school in recent times. We have really needed it, to make the decisions and take the steps we have taken.

For once, I don't need to cut a long story short, so I'll start with what happened last year. Mike came home one day (about September) and said he felt led to move to Canada. Then, within a couple of days his paths crossed with a couple of people whose interaction with him fuelled the idea. He said he wanted Deb and Joe to finish their education in Canada. I didn't really know how to respond, so we dropped it, except that he collected preliminary information and guidelines from the Embassy.

He also began to prepare his CV for approval by the relevant Canadian body, as recommended by the Embassy, as a prerequisite to a successful application. That took a lot of time and brought us to early 1999 without my getting too concerned about what was happening. In the meantime, I had the opportunity to share quite deeply with Sister Gloria Grey[1], and her ministry left me with a sense of a new day about to dawn for me personally. At the same time, I became very passionate (again) about interceding for Jamaica in the light of current and threatening crises, and developed a growing gut feeling that concerned Christians need to maintain an active presence in J. A.[2], rather than to find themselves elsewhere.

---

1.   An intercessor who ministered out of Trinidad, leading prayer and fasting retreats for churches.
2.   Jamaicans sometimes affectionately call the island "J. A.", or "Jam Down"

But early this year, Deb got involved in our deliberations, as she seemed to have received some personal revelation that we were indeed to go to Canada; and she got on our case every time we forgot about it. (She is very confident about nagging people 'in the Lord'.) So, our applications were submitted in March, naming just Mike, myself, Deb and Joe, as the others are over 19 years old, and Gail, who is still at (a US university), was not interested. I really became uneasy when I realized that this thing had not gone away, but it seemed possibly about to materialise, and I wrote to my cousins in Toronto and Ottawa to see whether they would be able to help us with the transition if it came to that. We received an interview date from the Embassy for the first of June, and by that time my gut reaction had just about reached my throat. It had really knotted me up inside. What would happen to the school? What would happen to my parents? How could we excuse ourselves from Jamaica at a time like this? What about Arianne? How could we leave her? How could we leave the British volunteers at the school, practically on their own? etc., etc.

So, I was really in prayer and fasting for much of May. In the middle of the month, I reluctantly went to a women's conference in Nashville with some of the Home Church sisters, at Pastor A's and Mike's suggestion, with the not-too-hidden agenda of soliciting support for the school. However, I had a really glorious time in the Lord. Some of the things Sister Gloria had told me would take place before the middle of the year began to happen there, and I was built up in faith to deal with the uncertainties we were facing. Shortly after we got back, God burdened Sister B with a concern for me, though she didn't know anything more than the general need of the school for more financial support. I was in Mandeville at a week-long Ministry of Education workshop, still fasting and praying privately about the various issues, when she called me late on the last morning, and told me she had been interceding for me since 3 a.m. I had also got up at 4 to pray, crying out to God to speak to me on these matters before I had to return to Kingston, later that day.

Sister B's call choked me up, as it was a complete surprise and I hadn't known of her concern. I was very blessed as she delivered God's answer, that although I had "looked to a group of people for help," and been disappointed because "they didn't see themselves as chosen," I should not worry because He was "raising up individuals" to help. She was not very much in the know, so I had to clarify what I had received: that I had made the expensive trip to Nashville to seek long- and short-term financing for the school, and returned empty-handed; but I should not worry because God had individuals who would take on the burden, who would see themselves as called to this work.

That was comforting, but what followed was a bit of a puzzle, as it said my family was actually more supportive than I thought.

I couldn't figure out that part, and wasn't free to take Sister B into my confidence, so she still did not know that there was anything but the school funding issue. We didn't speak for a couple of weeks, during which time the fear that moving to Canada may be moving out of the Lord's will did not go away. I came to the end of the month still troubled on that front, desperately asking God to shout His will at us in no uncertain terms, so I could know how to respond. On the last Sunday of May, Sister B came to me after church with another word from the Lord. She said her burden had not gone away either, and she had since had a vision in which Mike and the children were going in one direction, I was going in the opposite direction, and God was not pleased. The word of the Lord was that I should stop resisting, and fall in with the others. He also said that the other things I was thinking we should be involved in, were not for this time. I can't tell you how relieved I was to have the question settled, and my conscience clear.

The rest is just mundane: we went through three months of tedious red tape that tangled us into more-than-usual busyness, at the same time doing a lot of Mission School's work in preparation for leaving Mr. British Volunteer in charge for this year, as well as expanding the Nursery. During this time it became clear that the 'family' members (who were) very supportive of our initiative were the cousins in Ottawa, my parents, and the close Uncle and Aunt in Jamaica whom I would have to ask to 'look out for them.' Best Friend C and I prayed together a few times in August; and the last time, I saw a quick vision of a pair of hands covering something that looked like either a tiny pearl or a seed. The hands were just parted enough to allow a glimpse of it, and were cupped protectively around it, with the suggestion of being about to open slowly to show more of the object. This encouraged my 'waiting faith' again, to watch till the Lord chooses to unveil more of His work.

When they heard about our plans, some of the Home Church brethren were in shock, and you know that was not my doing. Left to myself, I would have chatted out everything long ago—uncertainties and all. So, here we are in Nepean (adjoining Ottawa). The children are in school, and Mike has returned home after landing us and spending two weeks. The 'plan' is for me to be here with Deb and Joe for a few months before he rejoins us. He and the other Elders have a lot going on, in addition to our personal affairs with all the strings attached. Please pray for him. Sean plans to marry Sarah in March; and Gail is currently doing a semester in Spain, after which she should spend Christmas to end-of-January in Jamaica, doing a Winter Study project before returning to (the U.S. university). These seem the only certainties in our agenda for the next six months. Everything else is still up in the air.

The cousin we are with is (real name and Jamaican claim to fame given). He and his wife, Claire, are being very hospitable, though we are quite a crowd and used to a lot of space. Chief Cousin is older than Mike and me, so only one of his sons is still at home, and only temporarily, which is what makes it possible at all. I am looking for a job with a Christian publisher (newspapers abound here) or one that will allow me time to free-lance as a Christian writer. I am not anxious to jump from one classroom situation into another, but have nevertheless applied for registration with the Ontario College of Teachers, a process which I'm told takes three months at least. I'm also going to spend some time catching up with the rest of the world in the areas where I've remained a non-starter, living and working at Mountain Village without even a normal phone all these years. Lesson 1 was the sending of email. If you have got this, it means I'm on to Lesson 2, and I would love to hear from you.

Mr. British Volunteer, who accepted the position of Mission School's Acting Principal until June 2000, may have sent you a current newsletter by now, if you are on his mailing list. If not, and you wish to hear how we got on this past academic year, or how you can help in the one just begun, please write to them as follows: ...
Love,
Evangeline

October 20, 1999

"Snail mail" to: Individual teachers at the mission school.
Dear Mrs C,

I hope, and have been praying, that all is well with you personally and with the school. Hope the term has so far been free of unpleasantness or injuries, and that you are all keeping good health—being strengthened in the Lord and in the power of His might, against illness and every other evil. Please say hello to your class and the parents for me—only Miss D's class[3] will wonder who she is talking about. Ask the children to remember to pray for me—their prayers of faith are very powerful.

---

3. New admissions in the Nursery

I have been well, though I have to be careful with the cold. We are already into gloves, socks, lined shoes, thermal underwear, and hooded wind-breakers with removable or replaceable inner jackets. The wind-breaker I have stops below the hips, and now I have to go and buy a nice coat that will go down to the ankles, because my legs get really cold if I'm on the road for a while, especially on windy days. Also, the real coat is more suitable for business wear than the wind-breaker, and I have been going about trying to establish a new source of income. I put it that way because I have been more keenly pursuing the publication of articles and attending job search workshops than actually looking for a job.

The past two mornings, I had to go to downtown Ottawa, and I hadn't done any weekend laundry, so I couldn't find suitable pants to wear. I had to wear ordinary, unlined skirts; and believe me—I'll never do it again. Though the skirts came almost to mid-calf and I wore them with long slips, the cold was bitter where the wind-breaker stopped. As a result of that, I got a bit feverish in the night. This also happens if I leave the window even slightly cracked to let in a little fresh air. In the middle of the night I would get awake with ague and it would take a lot of warming up before I stop shivering.

Also, when going about on foot, you need to carry a bag that can hang securely across your shoulders; so the hands can be free to be pushed into pockets, gloves and all, to keep warmer. I don't think this is any news to (the British teachers), but I met an English young lady at the CIDA[4] office on Monday, who said it gets much worse here than in England. I don't think I'll be here very long. It's only fall now: when we get to the real winter and the sort of weather she described to me, I'll write again and tell you about it, because I'm sure to be indoors most of the time....

(About taking the bus, etc.) ... Beside the driver is a machine that you drop your fare into, and it pushes out the ticket, which you just tear off. (You have to drop the right amount in coins, so this is a good way to get rid of loose change.) The fare is much more than in Jamaica, though. It's $2.25, which works out to about $56.25 Jamaican ... You can buy a one month or one year pass, and you can renew that original pass when it expires. It has your name and picture on it, and the time for which it is good, among other fine print. The school children and old people get theirs at a reduced rate, so I think it's a wonderful bus system...

---

4.   Canadian International Development Agency

There is a lot of glass in the buildings here, as they don't seem to have vandals who break things for fun. Some of the bus stops also have sides of glass, (the glass) going right around except for a small doorway, to protect people from the weather … Some only have a bench and a bus stop sign, but if you are at one like that, there is always a sheltered one up the road, where you could wait till your bus comes into view. The bus company is called OC Transpo; OC stands for Ottawa-Carleton … The shape of their normal buses is funny; the front looks like the back. However, they have some other buses called Para-transpo's, which are white, and look more like vans. Those transport people who are too handicapped to get on a normal bus, and to do this they have a platform that can go down to the ground from the doorway, to pick up and lift the person or wheelchair into the vehicle. To take these, you phone for the service or make a regular arrangement with them, rather than going to a bus stop. They come for you like a taxi.

This is necessary because many handicapped people have to go about their business just like other people. Yesterday, in the CIDA building, I saw a man with a tiny body in a very fancy wheelchair, zipping past me doing his executive job. His head looked very big, but I think it was because the body was so tiny. To get through the security door he just flashed something at it. He didn't have to go up to it and touch something like everyone else … To be unable to work in this country you either have to be totally lazy, sick in your head, or extremely, severely handicapped. Of course, it's not easy to get a well-paying job, and people do get laid off because of organizations 'downsizing' from time to time.

So, they have employment insurance for people who have lost their jobs, and a lot of sponsored training opportunities for people who need to be re-equipped for the changing job market. Of course, this is a very educated society, so every employer assumes literacy, most assume post-secondary education, and for good jobs, computer skills are needed and bilingualism (French and English) preferred. This is because Canada has two official languages, and the French speaking public is very mixed in with the English speakers. The minimum wage for adults is $6.85 per hour, which in Jamaica is $171 per hour, $1,368 per day, or $6,840 per week. So even if you can't get the job you want, you can't starve off a minimum wage job. There is a lower minimum for students (who work outside of school hours), and a lot of teenagers do. ... Deb and Joe are looking forward to doing that when they get used to 'the runnings'[5] here. ...

I should learn French and do some formal computer applications training... Meanwhile, the Ontario College of Teachers has to check out the qualifications of all teachers trained outside Ontario (not even just outside Canada) and certify them in order for them to work in a government school. I am doing some voluntary work now at a public school, helping one of the Special Education teachers two half days per week. This is because employers want you to have Canadian references, which I hope to get from the Principal here, and also because I want to get acquainted with their school system. So far, I have seen a lot of differences.

The money they have to spend is obviously many times more than we have in J. A. ... I won't bore you with describing the lovely school buildings and equipment. ... However, here are some of the differences. (1) They don't use the word 'and' in reading numbers. For example, 101 is read as "one hundred one". (2) At Deb and Joe's senior high school the (students) are allowed to smoke outside of lesson times, though the law says under-eighteens can't buy cigarettes. Then, the school turns around and offers programs to help the addicted ones to quit smoking. The (students) can speak to the teachers like their companions, and you have to be a really assertive adult to overcome this with ill-mannered children. Of course you can't (spank) them. However, the law doesn't prevent parents from spanking their own children, like in the US, and most Canadians are very polite, so you don't get many children with bad home training. ...   I'm trying to sell some writing to a...newspaper, and I need to fax and email some correspondence to them this morning, so that's it for now. God bless you, and continue to make you a blessing. There's a personal P.S. below, but the above is the same letter I wrote to all ...

Love,

Evangeline A.

---

[5] Jamaican slang for "the way of life."

October 24, 1999

"Snail mail" to: Household / farm employee

Dear Mrs. E,

I hope all is well with you, Mr. E, and the children ... I don't have any helper here, but I share the work with my cousin's wife. The children help a little too. The first time I washed some clothes, I didn't realize the water was so much hotter than at home, and one of Mr. Anderson's shirts shrank, so I had to give it to Joe ...

I had to buy a pair of lined boots to keep my feet and ankles warmer. It's not very pretty, because the pretty ones were more expensive, and Deb also needed one. ...

Deb and Joe are enjoying school. Deb has a friend who lives next-door ... and goes to the same school, so that girl is like (Deb's Jamaican best friend) now. Joe has put on weight. He got two bicycles from my cousins and repaired them himself, for the two of them to ride to school. They also ride if I send them to the supermarket or anywhere nearby ...

When I stand waiting for a bus, I have to (put) the wind-breaker hood over my head, close the flaps ... over the bottom part of my face, and draw the strings tight so that my cheeks are covered. Deb doesn't do so much because she doesn't feel as cold as I do, and she thinks it looks stupid. But she goes inside the bus stop to keep warmer, even if there are a lot of people in there already. Joe covers up like me. He doesn't feel 'any way.'[6]

I sent a long letter to the teachers at the school. Let (Mrs. F, your sister,) give you some of the other news, please. I don't want this letter to be too long. I sent Mr. Anderson a list of things I want you to pack for me, so that he can ship them or bring them with him when he and Ari are coming for Christmas. Please ask him for the list if he forgets to give it to you, and for boxes to pack then in ...

I dreamt about some people making a road through our land to go across to someone else's property. Please keep your eyes open against anyone using the place for a track. You must not allow this because it is dangerous. That's all for now. Hope you have a wonderful Christmas season when it comes.

Love,

Evangeline Anderson

---

6. Jamaican slang for "embarrassed".

November 12, 1999

"Snail mail" to: Best Friend, F.

Hi F,

Mike told me he gave you the urgent email. How are church life and (a named para-church organisation) going? (By the way, I need a reply to this letter; this is not only for occupational therapy.)

I miss all you brethren, but the atmosphere at Church # 3, where we are attending, is really good. They are into the scriptures, at least from the pulpit, almost as much as we are at Home Church ... The praise does not become frenzied like some of what I observed in Nashville, but young and old alike are very nimble on their feet and generally uninhibited ...

For Breaking of Bread they use unleavened 'bread' that looks like bits of soda biscuit to me, and dip this into one of the cups of wine that are held by the servers. So you don't even taste the wine, much less drink it, as the piece of biscuit is neither large nor absorbent. We have made friends with an English lady and her children who take us to the Sunday morning meetings ... I commented to her that it seems almost like a Roman Catholic scenario, but she said they started doing it that way to keep the 'Passover-like' significance that was shared with them by Messianic Jews.

I would much rather *break bread* and *drink* wine, but I suppose I'll live. Speaking of Messianic Jews, perhaps you didn't know, but I have been asking the Lord for years to bring me into close relationship with at least one who is a scholar, because I suspect that some unanswered questions I have could be helped by a Jewish perspective—or at least put to rest if I eliminate that possibility. Apart from which, I have been praying for the salvation of Jews for some time, and for the opportunity to help this along in some way. So, I located (a Messianic congregation) and am going to test the waters. They welcome Gentile visitors, but have some reservations about our 'charismatic' carryings-on. So I hear, anyway. I'll let you know how it goes.

I really have not been this free in years. I know it can't last too long, so I'm making the most of it while it does ... In case you think it's just me and the Lord, here is some proof that I'm paying attention to the mundane things. I'm back to doing my own housework, with less help from the youths than I would have if we weren't guests in someone's house—can't (be too stern with them) in public. I'm also house hunting, hoping to move by Christmas when Mike and Ari are supposed to come for two weeks. If the move doesn't work, we'll stay in an 'apartment hotel' for most of that time, so Chief Cousin can have space to entertain his own family. He has a son in Toronto, one in Alberta, and the youngest living in an apartment here, all of whom will be getting together at Christmas.

Deb and Joe are fine—getting good grades in grades 11 and 12 respectively. Joe's art is flourishing, and he's on the wrestling team. Believe it or not, Gym is a compulsory subject in Grade 11 … Deb got invited to the school's Leadership Training Camp up in some forested hill last weekend. The teachers selected her over many who have been around longer, so that was a big honor. On top of which she was the only black student among 35, and only the second selected from her year group. So, that's the bragging.

Back to new delights—God is so good. He is truly no man's (or woman's) debtor. I am in a setting here where people love to sing together. Chief Cousin and his wife Claire are choristers, and they love to sit around the piano and practice their hymns; so, now I have made it a trio, except that I'm getting them to sing choruses and the less doleful hymns. I found a song book here with the words to *almost* every song I ever wanted to know. When we celebrated Thanksgiving, the youths played Monopoly while we adults had a sing-along with one of Claire's choir sisters. She is a Jamaican with a very lovely voice, and a serious dedication to patois. Then, on Halloween, it was (the) birthday (of Jen and Chief Cousin's mom); and the birthday party ended in a sing-along too, at Jen's house with some of her church friends …

Deb and Joe are laughing at me, but I'm having a ball. They say you won't have the time to read such a long letter. A paragraph a day is fine—I'm making up for eight weeks. I have lost some weight by feasting on fruits a lot of the time, and my hair is growing very fast. On the other hand, there is acne out in full bloom on my face and I'm not sure why…

Last Sunday, I saw snow flurries for the first time, and on Friday night there was enough to settle on parked cars. I know it will get much colder, but I hear the weather warms up when it snows. Can't say I've noticed that so far. People suffer from a strange winter depression here, (attributed) to light deprivation. Already, it's dark by 5 p.m. and not dawn until about 7 a.m. The flocks of migrating birds have gone by, and the trees are all bare. The whole process is fascinating to watch …

The Lord has said a few specific things to me in morning devotions since I've been here. One morning I felt I had been (saying) too much without hearing any response, so I quieted myself and asked God to talk back to me. Guess what He said? A very suspect 'word': "I love you." Out of the blue, as plain as day and ridiculously simple. Another time, I got concerned that

I hadn't been praying for anyone, but just rejoicing in the Lord, so I asked specifically for a burden[7] to intercede for whoever was in need. Up to that point I hadn't remembered it was the day that Friend G's husband was to have shared his heart with the members; but then, a terrific burden and (spiritual) warfare leading came, about their situation. I received a specific 'word' (I believe, of wisdom), so I called Pastor A and told him before he left home for the meeting.

Then, on the morning of the Bawl-out[8], I was about to start praying for Jamaica when the Lord said, "Give me space!" The area available to me in the basement is fairly small, but the instruction was so clear that I started to push things further back to allow more space, before starting to worship. Well, in doing that, I got near to a bookshelf and was drawn to a certain book. When I pulled it out, it was a book of testimonies[9] written by a Jamaican mother, Gloria Grant, who ... used to be on staff at the UWI[10]. They were testimonies of supernatural intervention in her daily family life, told in a very matter-of-fact way that gave total tribute to God. That got me reflecting on the value of our Jamaican Christian experience. The next thing was that I was led to select Lester Lewis's[11] music, instead of some of the tapes I usually put in the walkman to rejoice with. That led me into such a war dance, it wasn't funny. Then, when I was praying, God gave me a word of encouragement for Lester; so again I called Pastor A and asked him to relay it.

Less than a month before we left Jamaica, the Lord woke me up one morning with these words: "I am going to circumcise the foreskin of your circumstances." You may remember me asking you at Church about all the benefits of physical circumcision ... as I was trying to figure out this weird

---

7. Jargon in some Christian circles, meaning "a compelling urge to pray", or "a compelling concern".

8. Jamaican slang for "cry loudly," used to title a "National Day of Repentance" organized by several churches and convened at the National Stadium in Kingston, on October 16, 1999. Press reports said that Governor-General Sir Howard Cook "led the charge" at the stadium, "in an emotionally charged address," and "told the thousands gathered that his prayers were for him to set a good enough example ... so others would follow ... in turning to the Almighty for guidance." Sunday Herald, October 17, 1999.

9. *Flush, in Jesus' Name! ... and Other Stories*, by Gloria Grant

10. University of the West Indies, where F, the addressee of this letter, was a medical doctor on staff.

11. A Jamaican pioneer in reggae gospel music, who was headlining the band performances at the 'Bawl-out'.

sentence. Well, after a while I thought it was talking about cutting away things that were preventing a necessary expansion, and this is really taking place. I also thought it referred to cutting away things that fostered 'germs,' and this may involve more than I have seen already. But praise God, and may His will prevail.

There was another unsolicited word God dropped on me several months ago, about personal financial blessing, which I see no sign of at the moment. I am praying for an 'entrance' into the world of Christian journalism / writing / editing ... which will be profitable enough to allow me to do it full time. All the advice I have had from people in the field is negative on this, but I am appealing to God to gainsay this and give me the outcome no-one else thinks is likely ...

...(Report on the progress of a very ill cousin, for whom Home Church intercessors had been asked to pray) ... I think this is enough for now. Please cheer up Mike for me ... Blessings and greetings for all and sundry. Bye for now.

Love,

Evangeline

January 8, 2000 6:23 a.m.

Email To: Home Church brethren in Jamaica and the US

Hi, you lovely people!

Happy New Year if I haven't been in touch recently. It's not belated, as we perhaps have over 11 months to go. Thanks for the messages / letters I have been getting through Mike. I will remember to pray for all your ministries ... May God use you in 2000, in ways that *feel* just as worthwhile as you know by faith that His service is. And may your communion with Him be such that you will hear His personal commendation, especially if you get negative vibes from elsewhere, in response to doing His will.

I sent a long letter to F with Mike when he went home on Jan. 3rd, telling about our moving, and how the Lord has set us up in this new home. It was *part* of the testimony of the moment. Here is a synopsis of that, and also the rest, starting with things I have fully learnt.

- God answers prayers: when, how, and with what adjustments He chooses! He edits according to His foreknowledge to give us the best, which our limited vision may not have discerned, or our limited boldness and 'God-concept' could not conceive or articulate in prayer.

- God *sometimes* weaves the prayers of His people together to answer in a single tapestry, even when they don't seem to be totally agreed except for the genuine, "Thy will be done!"

- God stores up prayers, and *sometimes* deals with them by number (take a number and wait till it's called!) That's not "take a number among other people," but "take a number among your own prayers over the years."

- At other times, He prioritises them according to urgency, knowing the circumstances in which we live, and knowing the effects of certain factors better than we do. So, He protects us.

- Overall, He orchestrates events so that His actions benefit *all* His children. He does not play favorites, though it sometimes seems that way temporarily; or though Satan's lying spirits who attend Self-pity may whisper otherwise.

These were my *personal*, stored-up prayers, with which I either came to Canada, or spent the first three months praying:

1. For *more* devotional time, and opportunity for *freedom* with the Lord.

2. For a break from teaching ...

3. For opportunity to *write* and have published: current Christian commentary, uplifting stuff, as well as the inspiring experiences of the past years.

4. For this to prove financially rewarding—i.e. a writing job... which allows time for free-lance work; or enough free-lance work to live off...

5. For involvement with Jews; this has been a leading of the Spirit in my heart for some time.

6. (Sep. to Nov.) For a *suitable* place to *rent* ASAP, as my cousin's house was brimming over with us...

Mike agreed with all these in principle, but felt more urgency than I did, for me to widely job hunt without being too selective, to be employed before trying to move, and to be open to purchasing rather than renting.

7. (Nov. to Dec.) For my certification to teach here, and the application process, started before leaving J. A, to come through from the Ontario authority. (By this time I had concluded that I'd better get back into teaching, for the freedom of the holidays, the steady income, and the obvious legitimacy of being out at work.)

8. (Nov. to Dec.) For our negotiations about housing to work out without implicating anyone else as surety; since we have no one here who could fully agree in faith with us.

9. (Nov. to Dec.) For my menstrual cycle to settle down, especially for Mike's visit to be as pleasant as possible for the Christmas / New Year holiday.

So these were the prayers. Observe God's answers and plot His priorities.

#1. 'Called.'[12] I have had the best devotional time ever, except when I was at home for two years at Mona, ending in Deb's birth and our move to Mountain Village. It turns out Jen was diagnosed with Cancer in October ... Since we came here in September, we have been close ... She feels that God sent me here to be with her, and much of my intercessory energy has been spent on her. (Some notable time on Jamaica also) ... I have grown in fasting, and really touched the electrifying hem of His garment on some of those fasting occasions.

#2. 'Called.' The applications I sent out to schools, just in case I was misreading God's timing, were unsuccessful without the Ontario certification ... So, I have had three months' break, except for a few days' volunteer work at a school to get acquainted with the system.

#3. Partly 'called,' hopefully to be 'called' again. I have been writing for (a monthly tabloid) ... but this is not paid work, and only one or two articles per month. I also accepted the part time job of advertising salesperson ... Earnings are strictly commission-based, and I am new to sales and Ottawa, so it has been rather dismal. You can't be employed in mainstream journalism here without a journalism degree, and I have only had one article accepted by a paying paper. Obviously, there are things to learn about getting published, and I am learning; so I'll keep trying.

#4. Still to be 'called.'

#5. 'Called' in stages. First, it turned out that the Senior Pastor of Church # 3 keeps a burden for the Jews at the forefront of the fellowship's concerns. I

---

12. That is, the number taken for waiting in turn has been "called."

searched the web and found a Messianic fellowship in this city, but … far away from where we were, and I have not been able to visit. Then, God arranged for (a new church 'sister', H) to become attached to us … She turned out to have a deep burden for the Jews, and to be teaching at a Jewish school here. When I told her about the Fellowship I had found on the web, she said she had visited it, identified for me the area where it was, and encouraged me. Then, when we started investigating the 'new' house (see below), I discovered it was near to the Messianic meeting place, and also neighbored by a Jewish residential area.

I told her we were moving to (that area) and may attend (a named church nearby) for commuting convenience, and she gave me the contact numbers for a 'sister' there, who is actively carrying the same burden in that church, although the church has not institutionalised it. In the move, I lost the numbers, and was on the verge of asking H for them again. Yesterday I prayed, "Lord, now that I have completed the moving assignment, and been waiting so long to follow this desire, please arrange for me to visit the Messianic fellowship's Friday evening prayer meeting. I will get there by bus or on foot, but please arrange a drive home in the cold for me."

Lo and behold, I got an evening call from the lady whose numbers I had lost. She had decided to make the first approach, since H had told her of me but she had not heard from me. When I told her of my desire for the evening, she said the Friday meeting was off for this week, but she would pick me up for the Saturday Bible Study today. Isn't God good?

#6, 8 'Called,' and superseded by God's 'better.' A deal on renovated town homes jumped at me out of the paper, one day in late October. We visited the site, I called Mike, and we applied against the odds of our non-credit-rating in Canada. Five weeks and a few mortgage financiers later, it was tied up and we got the keys on December 17th. The broker we ended up with was very good, working with us till she found a solitary Quebec company that would deal with our unusual circumstances, at a % deposit and interest rate we could live with. We shunned every opportunity to be deceptive (they were slyly suggested by various people), and to ask help of relatives …

#7 'Called,' only in the New Year's week, after the whole move was over. If this had come earlier, I would not have had the time to do all the phoning, faxing, real estate office and lawyer visits that secured the house. Now I have submitted my papers to the District School Board, and soon they should have me on a list to the schools for substitute teaching … In early December, when I was getting desperate about employment, God told me to walk a section of (a named road close to home). I did that, and it was a very long walk. The significant places I saw were three schools, the District Board office, a Pentecostal church, and the convenience stores. At the Pentecostal church, they referred me to a Christian School I had not known was nearby (2 buses), and I went there before returning to (the named road). There, I had the most positive reception, got called in by the Acting Principal the following day for an interview, and was put on their substitute teachers list till they have an opening.

#9 'Called, most spectacularly. I told Mike, God really loves him! I couldn't believe the extremes that sorted themselves out in my circumstances and body in November / December. First, the Evening Primrose Oil that I had been taking religiously for months got finished, and with all that was going on, I forgot to unpack and start the next bottle—you know about me and tablets. Then, ovulation symptoms I had not *felt* in months hit me, followed over the next fortnight by pre-menstrual symptoms I had also not *felt* in months—not all unpleasant, just very marked. (I didn't fuss with anyone, believe it or not.) The Lord stretched out the cycle to exactly four weeks, with the brawta[13] that libido came into its own! I had to include this testimony—hope it blesses you.

Please pray for us when you remember, and for Mission School's headship to be taken over fully by the right people. Much love and blessings to you and family.
Evangeline

February 6, 2000, 6:23 a.m.

Email to: Mike, Ari, Gail and Pastor A
Hi All,

Just an exciting bulletin on Deb and Joe. They have been attending a youth conference at Church #3 the past two evenings, and came back positively bubbling last night. They have received the Baptism in the Holy Spirit (or the evidence in Deb's case, as she thinks she received before, from Pastor A's ministry) … we were up very late as they filled me in on every detail of all that went on. The person ministering was an Elijah type—they found him kind of scary. He not only (addressed) specific people on various issues,

---

13. Jamaican Creole for 'bonus,' or 'something given in addition to what was expected.'

but gave stern warnings to others about what would be happening to them in a few weeks / months, if they ignored the call to … acknowledge their condition and receive ministry. He was dealing mostly with immorality, drug abuse, witchcraft, and people leading double lives in the church. A lot of the immorality being dealt with was through Internet use…

Now Deb and Joe have got down from their 'spectator' perch at this new church, for which I am overjoyed. They told me they were 'jumping' (Deb's high heels very wisely discarded) and she was skinning even more teet'[14] than usual. I am still not over the virus, so I stayed home … I hope to go with them to the final meeting. Hope you have a good day to start a good week. 'Bye for now.

Love,

Evangeline

April 28, 2000

Fax to: The Editor, *The Gleaner* (edited version was published in May and posted by residents in the square of Mountain Village).

Madam Editor:

I am writing in support of the (Mountain Village) Community Action Group, in the public airing of their concerns via an open letter to Mr. Errald Miller, which you published on April 28. I was resident in (Mountain Village) for over 16 years, and have been hearing this annual story of telephone service being supplied 'next year' or 'by year-end', for all that time. In fact, if my memory serves me correctly, the citizens who spearheaded the initial petitions and the surveying of prospective customers, which Jamaica Telephone Company used to put back on their shoulders, are now either dead, or have passed the struggle on to those who have not yet given up.

Congratulations to the present Community Action Group. I laud their going public with this grouse. They have neither exaggerated the facts, nor the perceptions within the community that we have been disadvantaged for political or socio-economic reasons. I think those who drafted the letter were unnecessarily humble, in conceding that their thoughts may be ill-founded, and suggesting that someone 'important' needs to move into the area, in order for something as basic as telephone service to be warranted. Even in terms of the suggestion regarding cordless phones, Cable and Wireless needs

---

14.   Jamaican slang, to "skin one's teet" (teeth), means to grin.

to convince people like us that they are considering all their options, if they really expect to regain any credibility.

Allow me to inform the misinformed that there are some very important people living in (Mountain Village). World famous Blue Mountain Coffee, a product to which we can all still attach national pride—in grasping at untarnished emblems—is grown there, by people who need to maintain contact with those who prosper from their labour, drink the coffee, balance the budget with the help of foreign exchange earned, and supply goods / services to clients in (Mountain Village).

Then, there are the very important youth, not all of whom are happy to be forced into city dwelling, leaving family provisions behind in these hard times. Jamaica stands to lose untold potential by neglecting them. Their caregivers need telephones for emergencies that threaten child survival, and they themselves will need community Internet access, just like the students who live a stone's throw away in Kingston. The one public call box, which is so often out of order, cannot suffice. Only the truly idle can loiter in the square at the end of a queue to make a call.

Also resident in (Mountain Village) are those whom the nation itself has acknowledged as important, some of whom have served well in high-profile roles. I will not call names and violate people's privacy, but one wonders whether politics does play a part in their relative importance not bringing the simple convenience of telephone service to the area. Is Cable and Wireless one long arm of a system that punishes those who serve, by forcing them to serve at their own expense, paying through their noses for cellular phones to support the job functions by which they serve the public? I do believe the Community Action Group may not be too far off, in suggesting that Cable and Wireless' profiteering from its few cellular clients is more lucrative than the provision of ordinary community-wide service would be. But is their mission to serve the country, or to rip off those whom they possibly can?

The serene beauty of (Mountain Village) has long attracted tourists, and the potential for booming eco-tourism is there. Admittedly, groups such as the Community Action Group would need to work hard at hospitality training among the most disenchanted, but telephone service is an absolute pre-requisite for eco-tourism and its foreign exchange proceeds to materialise.

I just pray that before this Community Action Group grows too weary in well-doing, there will be normal telephone service in (Mountain Village).

And if they have to make some noise in the ears of (those pretending to be deaf), my prayers are there with them too.

I am

M. E. Anderson ...

June 7, 2000

"Snail mail" to: Graduating class of Mission School.

Hi Grade 6!

I felt I had to write to you before you all leave for different places in a few weeks time. I hope you have all had a very blessed year together, and that the GSAT[15] results will reward everyone for the work they put in.

There are many reminders here that prevent me from forgetting Mission school. For example, I have been teaching a few hours a week at an after school learning centre off (a road named) 'Conroy'. So, I remember Conroy (your schoolmate) very often. Then, last week I taught a public school class with a girl named Stacey-Ann Ellis. I could hardly believe it, but I told her about 'my' Stacey-Ann. This girl didn't look like Stacey-Ann, though. She looked almost like Ebony's biggest sister.

When the students here are showing how rude they can be, I compare their behaviour with the Mission School students, and realize that you are much better off. Although you don't have all the fancy stuff they have to use in the classroom, you have the attitudes that will allow God to bless you. Here, (teachers) can't call God's name in the schools, so it's no wonder that some classes are so terrible.

The news here has been reporting on several children and students dying recently. One high school had two. One boy fell overboard into the river during an end-of-year party his graduating class held on a boat. They were drinking... and he was... doing handstands on the railing. (Minors—people under the age of 18—are prohibited by law from drinking, and we all know that no-one should ever drink till they are drunk.) Another boy from the same school fell off an artificial mountain. It was at the cinema where he worked part time, and they had set up the mountain to advertise a movie. No-one was supposed to climb it without 'straps', but he was disregarding that rule.

---

15. Grade Six Achievement Test, a national exam by means of which students are assigned high school places. Jamaican high school starts with Grade 7.

So, it seems to me that you children are very blessed to have been taught to obey. If you are obedient you will be spared many dangers, because the adults who make the rules know the dangers better than you. Please remember that, as you graduate and go off to high schools. Also, if you are known as a 'good' girl or a 'good' boy, then, when things happen that are beyond your control, you will get more support.

I am praying that you will also remember to stay out of bad company. God is not pleased when we take pleasure in the company of wrong-doers (Romans 1:32), whether it's at school, on the street, or on the bus. Wherever they are carrying on their misbehaviour, make sure you are far away! The only way it is right for you to stay there, is if you are correcting them and they seem to be listening to you. If they are not going to listen, then you leave them, or you may be entangled in the web when they are caught. These things happen in high schools much more than at Mission School).

Have a wonderful summer too, and help your parents as much as you can. Let them feel appreciated for all the effort and sacrifice they will have to keep putting into your education. And do your best not to disappoint them, please! Many parents (especially the mothers) suffer from heartache and heart-break if their children let them down, or behave in an ungrateful way.

Well, I wish you all a wonderful set of GSAT results, and a memorable graduation and prize-giving ceremony. I hope to hear many good things about your progress in the future. See, you have my address, so I look forward to some replies. God bless you.

Love,

Evangeline Anderson

Letter published in *The Gleaner*, July 4, 2000

Captioned: "The sacrifice of volunteers"

The Editor, Madam:

For volunteer work in an Ottawa school, assisting the Special Education teacher seven hours per week from October to December 1999, I was surprised to receive very flattering acknowledgment. Of course, I expected to be thanked when I had to withdraw, but to my mind, those gracious words were the natural end of the matter. I'd had my own reasons for volunteering, and also realized that my brief service was just a drop in the bucket for that teacher I had been helping.

Months later, while gazing through a bus window on a city-centre route, I read in bold letters on a bill-board, "We love our Volunteers." Even then I only wondered dimly what that new sign was about. Soon, I realized from a radio broadcast that it was Volunteers' Week in Ottawa, when various institutions joined in city-wide acknowledgment of their volunteers' indispensable service.

Days afterward, I received a phone call from OCRI, the city agency administering the Volunteers in Education program, and was actually embarrassed to confirm that I had only served till December. Yet, soon there was, waiting for me at the school concerned, a monogrammed copy of OCRI's publication 'Thank You to the Volunteers,' with my name included in a center-spread list, as well as an invitation to various events planned to fete volunteers. Icing on the cake was the school's subsequent invitation to a Volunteers' Brunch, which unfortunately I had to miss in pursuit of paid employment.

All of which brings me to this point. In Jamaica, we too benefit from the service of Volunteers, though without a public organization devoted to administering their affairs. Their service is not widely acknowledged, often rendered unto man as unto God, with assurance only of His reward. Another difference in Jamaica is that most volunteers seem to be expatriates, as we very rarely find it in our hearts to bestow such sacrifice on our own people (outside of the religious orders).

Our schools, in particular, have benefited from expatriate volunteers; and Mission School in (Mountain Village), rural St. Andrew, is one such. Since 1989, this young school has only been able to offer worthy service to (Mountain Village) through the utilization of volunteer teachers, our designation of 'volunteer' meaning one who offers to serve at a fraction of the regular cost. This has always meant sacrifice on their part—sacrifice of at least a year of their lives, as well as significant potential income.

I am happy to say that three of Mission School's volunteers have been Kingstonians, which shows that there are still Jamaican lay people who will consider that level of sacrificial service. One of these served almost at the expense of professional standing among her colleagues in a very prestigious profession. Jamaican charitable institutions need more of our own who are willing to sacrifice chunks of their time in this way.

Nine of Mission School's volunteers have, however, hailed from the United Kingdom—on top of all else, sacrificing the First World comfort zone to which they were accustomed. Many volunteer agencies have struck Jamaica off their list of destinations because of our social climate; therefore, some of our volunteers came even without the support of such agencies. These young people deserve highest commendation, and the thanks of the whole Jamaican community, as well as the individuals they served.

I am, etc.,

M. E. Anderson…

September 26, 2000, 1:07 p.m.

Email to: Home Church brethren.

Hi there!

In customer service, Ottawa style, you don't greet people with "Hello," or "Hi," or even "Good Morning." You say, "Hi there!" And it must be as chirpy as you can make it, regardless of the face you see before you.

Well, totally out of character, I have had to be 'turning mi mout' mek fashion.'[16] What a thing to learn! That was one of the most annoying things about supply teaching in the younger grades—if I didn't try to sound like a Canadian, the kids couldn't understand me. So, there I was, finding myself automatically twangin'[17] for survival. *Ah couldn' recognise mi own voice.* Embarrassing!

Right now, Mike is on a one-week course in Montreal … Deb and Joe are fine, and back at school (Grade 13 and 12 respectively). Joe got into a 'co-op' course at school, but not the one he wanted. Co-op is an option where you get a taste of the working world—½ day school, ½ day work for a semester. In high school you don't get paid for it, but in college and university you do … He wanted the experience in a drafting or architectural firm, but … he ended up as an art teaching assistant to 9th and 10th graders at a different high school.

By the way, congrats to you all, on the excellent Olympic team! Deb and Joe are downstairs making a lot of noise in front of the TV, over their performance. Deb is also going through the throes of deciding which universities to apply to, what she wants to study there, and what is the most fool-proof way of lining up herself this year for whatever scholarships / bursaries she can get. … (Because of an irregularity that the school is blaming on a computer failure over the holidays), she wasn't able to get into an English

16. Adapted from the Jamaican Creole phrase, "tun yu 'an mek fashion", meaning "using whatever you have available, to create what you want, need, or what others will accept." The original context is that of someone creating a fashionable garment out of something that is not.

17. Jamaican slang for 'trying to speak with a North American or British accent.'

course she should be taking, so she and her best friend took the option of doing it at night school—6 to 9:30 p.m., two days per week. To cope with this, she had to give up her evening job, but she is still on call for Saturdays, as caregiver to a Down's Syndrome patient she took on over the summer.

We have had some struggles since you saw me in July, but God has His ministers at the right places and times to prevent us from shouldering what we can't bear. Our biggest challenge has been concern over Ari's and my parents' welfare. But no matter how hard I try, I can't find a verse to justify worry. (Of course, I also try to call it something else at times.) The truth is, if you do what you should when you should, there will be less temptation to worry. Isn't hindsight a wonderful thing? I also remember F's sharing, over a year ago, about the futility of 'un-prayed prayers,'[18] so I try not to fall into that trap.

I have been keeping in touch with J (a mutual friend who is a new immigrant in Toronto), by phone. She got a job in a miraculously short time, also with a bank, and I have felt privileged to share some tips with her, just in terms of the different job culture here. When you are not aware of certain differences, even in the employment lingo, amusing and not-so-amusing misunderstandings arise. Anyway, she is fine after her second week at work. We compare notes on the myriad of transactions there are to be learnt, the new (paperless) banking computer system, training, staff attitudes, etc. We both have trouble with the coins, and you'd better believe it—Canadians respect their coins just as much as their bills. No one feels too 'big' to arrive with a bag full of coins for you to change to bills, or deposit. They can buy wrappers at the (store) or get them at the bank; so some arrive with them well packaged, but some don't....

(Update on the progress of our appeal, on behalf of Mission School, for funding from a Christian organisation here ... Update on Jen's condition, for Home Church intercessors had been asked to pray for her.)

Mike is more comfortable at Church # 3 than he was at first, and the children have had a roaring-good summer of youth group interaction. (Swimming, sleeping over, horse-back riding, touring, etc. Unfortunately, no outreach.) Deb also has her Muslim school friend asking endless questions about Jesus, and wrestling with the answers ...

Well, whatever else has been happening on our side is just too mundane to write about. How about your news?...How are your local church outreach

---

18.   Prayers you talk about praying, intend to pray, but never do.

efforts going?… And, F, I'm still curious. You haven't answered my 'facety'[19] questions.

One voice has been telling me that you people must be vexed with me about something, and that is why the silence is so deafening. Another voice says you are all just extremely pressured and don't need any diversion from the job of keeping body and soul together. Am I getting warm? Or is there some less likely explanation?

Bless the Lord, brethren. And God bless you too.

Love,

Evangeline

February 11, 2001, 8:43 a.m.

Email to: (Dr. G G, New Board Chairperson of Mission School, who is also a friend, and Home Church member.)

Dear G,

We got your email on Friday night, but I was too tired to think straight. On Saturday mornings I do an accounting class … In the afternoon I had to sort the past year's documents, as it's tax return time here. Everyone over 18 is supposed to file returns. Praise the Lord, I got a good rest last night and had a lovely dream about Mission School's students and parents. … **(Dream related, leading to the following comments)**…

May God in His mercy prevent Mission School from 'borrowing' anything from the non-Biblical world view, as there is no benefit in it. The Kingdom (of God) *is* about *quality* of life, as opposed to what the world has to offer. So, I will be praying earnestly for your Board meeting … Mission School is guided by the philosophy of Christian Education, and the realities of the rural, socio-economic, and religious nature of our target population. It's a different culture from the uptown J. A., or the North American; and what works with them won't necessarily work at Mission School. The only guarantees come with the word of God, which is why I stuck with that.

I think it's a blessing that (a newly recruited Canadian donor) might bring A Beka supplies for you, as it would be really good to have the maximum Christian curriculum input throughout the school. What inhibited that all

---

19. Jamaican Creole, meaning 'feisty'

along was funding, and the Common Entrance[20] (examination), as parents could easier afford the J. A. books which were geared specifically toward that exam. It remains to be seen whether God is arranging continuing (new donor) support with A Beka books; but I know the whole package is still too expensive for the general population in Mountain Village to afford, because they may still need the specifically GSAT-oriented books.

Remember, the aim is to lift a whole community out of (adversity)— not only a few bright or privileged individuals ... By the way, (a named learning-disabled student) *has* been learning. He has learnt civility, life skills like keeping clothes on, keeping himself dry, socially acceptable behaviour, etc. If Mrs. C and Miss D should tell you what that child used to do when he ... came to Mission School, before he learnt all these things, you would think they were joking. So, his school fees have been justified like everyone else's. Academically, there has been a ceiling on his life, but otherwise, he has made wonderful progress that wouldn't have happened anywhere else without Special Education.

But enough of that! Congrats on your (and Coach K's) ... success with the team! And God bless you for your continuing (care for) these children. You deserve all the prayers you can get ...

'Bye,

Evangeline

February 12, 2001

"Snail mail" to: Relatives and friends.

Hi (So and so),

I feel as if the address here should be North Pole Street. This place is so cold, it's a shame. Mike's adopted sister ... who lives in New Jersey, claims that only mad people live 'up there' (where we are). Of course, those born here didn't have a choice, but the other day I heard Mike asking himself what on earth *he* is doing here. I didn't bother to kimbo[21] and say, "Ah really wanda!"[22]

Last winter, everyone here said it was a very mild winter. It was our first; so, to me there was nothing mild about it. Plus, without a car we had

---

20. Pre-cursor of the GSAT examination. See footnote, page 124.
21. Jamaican Creole, meaning 'put one's hands on the hips,' in what is often perceived as an argumentative stance.
22. "I really wonder!"

maximum exposure on the road. Therefore, I really felt proudly tough, that we managed so well. And I really thought we had been 'seasoned' to the Ottawa winter. So, this year should have been no problem.

But the weather authorities are confirming that it has been the worst in at least five years. Since mid-December, it started with a big snow storm that cancelled school and embarrassed (Ottawa's) snow removal machinery. I sent Ari some pictures from the press coverage of that week. A few days later, several more inches came down, and so on, straight to the end of January ...

The road accidents have been frequent and deadly. Just last weekend, there was a bad chain-reaction one caused by a sudden 'white out'. That's a blinding of motorists by very heavy snowfall (or wind-blown snow). But the worst thing for householders has been the burden of ice and snow on the roofs. Some that didn't leak last year are now leaky ... Praise God, we don't (have leaks), but we had to have a contractor clean the snow and ice off last week, as the weight can cause other damage, and the icicles hanging down over our front door were long and dangerous. After the workmen were finished, there was more than four feet of snow in our backyard, evenly spread. The guys had cleared the front door, but Joe and Mike had to dig and shovel for quite a while to clear the back door and the basement window.

This may sound exciting, but it's not. Last week, the weather warmed up a bit, only to have freezing rain instead of snow. The kind of rain that falls at just around zero temperatures ... It freezes on everything it touches. If you have a big beard it may freeze on your beard. It freezes on the branches, the vehicles, etc. Everyone dreads it...because pathways and roads become smoothly iced over and more treacherous. The snow banks also get glazed over with ice.

The crews have to go out before day, and spread more salt and coarse sand than they normally do, just so people can go to work (if they have to). They do the sidewalks, paths and roads. The salt melts the ice and the sand provides some traction. That's why I could make it to the bus stop and to work on Friday. And yet, some others (Canadians!) did not turn up because they were scared to drive ... It's so easy to fall and get hurt. Two of my co-workers have been seriously injured this season. Both Joe and I have fallen today, for the first time this year. Fortunately, he's athletic and I'm well padded.

He has got over the pneumonia and is back in circulation. The curfew we had to put on him has been lifted, as we have no more excuse. It still gets dark early ... so when he and Deb go out with their friends in the evenings, there are several hours of darkness before they turn up. I think I'm improving with the worry syndrome, or maybe I'm all worried-out.

Deb's foot is healing, but she is still under observation because it is still a bit painful. We have a clinic and a hospital near us. We don't pay for X-rays, blood tests, or examinations—only prescriptions. Of course, the doctors have all the equipment you see on 'ER,'[23] but they don't impress me as being as good at diagnosis as our J. A. doctors. If the equipment and tests can't spell it out for them, 'you salt'[24] ...

I can't hog this computer any more tonight. Mike is waiting patiently to get on. So, that's it for the weather-related update for you people in warmer places ...

Love,

Evangeline

February 19, 2001, 9:21 a.m.

Email to: Best friend F

Hi F,

I'm replying to a letter that was not sent to me. But heck, who can wait on the right letter? (Like the new lingo? Joke! That was only for effect.) Since Gail came back (to the US from a visit to Jamaica), no one in J. A. has written us except for three lines from Brother L, and Mission School business from G and (the new principal) M). Hint, hint!

...I'm 1½ courses into a ... Certificate in Bookkeeping ... God knows, I had enough 'bookkeeping' practice at Mission School, bungling a lot because I didn't know how to do it properly. Next time, I will. I have been finding the courses very interesting (and amusing against the background of Mission School experience). Also challenging, as work at the bank has been leaving me with less and less energy for study or assignments.

The past few weeks at work have been very unpleasant, the new ... supervisor being a very unreasonable and abrasive person—even with customers—which backfires on us lower life forms, as we get all the blame for people being turned off.

Otherwise, life is O.K. Walking the thin line between permissiveness and over-protectiveness in ... parenting teens continues to be a challenge, and

---

23. Popular Emergency Room television series.
24. Jamaican slang meaning, "You are out of luck."

the line is thinner on this side of the ocean. The society does not recognise 'protectiveness' of over-18s, but regards it more as dictatorship and interference with legally independent persons. So, even the under-18s are a bit touchy about parental restraints, and it's a very contagious disease.

Anyway, Deb and Joe are O.K … Joe's giftedness in Art got him a special feature in the yearbook. Deb just got a job as Youth Worker at the YMCA— for as many evening and weekend hours per week as studies will permit. She has yet to finalise the schedule with her boss. But she has the (advantage), as they really want her. She had another good offer, which they knew about. She gets glowing recommendations from the teachers at school, and does very well at interviews.

(A named university) is also keeping in closer touch with her than the others she applied to. Most likely, each does the same with the applicants in its territory. It's a thing with organisations up here—there is no waiting period to get responses from them, and they keep it coming, till you are either enlisted or eliminated.

Joe is having a wonderful life—not a care in the world … His focus is on his social life, which is narrowing down in a certain direction. Saturday night, the last bus coming our way almost left him stranded, as he left his favorite haunt (and 'best friend') on the other side of the city too late, and then wasted some time by taking the wrong bus and getting lost. Anyway, I was too tired to wait up, so I said, "God, is your 'pickney' tonight!"[25]

Sunday morning, I saw his giant shoes blocking the middle of the hallway, and (through his door) the pants thrown down over the pile on a chair, so I didn't need to look in the bed to make sure he was there. They are … good kids anyway, just overly optimistic about what to expect from life …

How are your three doing? Gail told us about her bawling / sharing the other day. She thought we would have got many reports about it, but L only wrote, "Gail cried and shared at church today."[26] Of course, I got more of the story from Ari…

She is quite cheered up now, getting grad school interviews at an encouraging rate, etc. And we trust the Lord to make all things beautiful (even our bungling) in His time. Please greet (your husband) Brother N and

---

25. "Lord, he is your child tonight."
26. She was crying about the home base having been moved to Canada, leaving her very little to come home to in Jamaica, and triggering an identity crisis.

the youths for me. Hope you are seeing God's goodness at all times, even through the clouds.

Much love,

Evangeline

May 4, 2001

"Snail mail" to: Friends and relatives in Jamaica

Dear (So and so),

Hope you're feeling very blessed, as well as knowing by faith that you are. A little feeling goes a long way. The Lord has been good to us since I last wrote a long praise report, and I started drafting one at work, as home time is short. Friday is my longest lunch break (1 hour), and it sure doesn't take all that time to eat …

After a long, harsh winter that broke snowfall records for some provinces, we are now in the middle of spring. But nature has been a bit confused, and giving summer temperatures too soon. This week we had the hottest 1st and 2nd May on record (30+ degrees C). It was windy though, so the effect was balmy, like a cool night out at Harbour View Drive-In.[27]

(In Mike's new job, things are not always smooth), but God showered the company recently with new contracts … They are also attracting new investors, so things are going better there. If only the two top guys could co-operate more … all would be rosy for Mike in his middle management role.

Anyway, he's living a blessed life. Most weekdays after work he relaxes by watching taped episodes of—get this—Startrek! To each his own, I suppose. For me, times of quietness are to be grasped, so I usually retreat while Startrek takes its course. I have been thanking God for all the learning opportunities He has provided for me here. And the old brain has not been doing badly. Mastering certain job skills in this high-tech banking environment has really been satisfying, and I think I have learnt fast, considering that in J. A. I had serious computer phobia. (It's hard on the eyes, though, or in my case I should say, the eye.) My mind still has difficulty getting around the concepts of this high finance business … especially as they relate to Biblical ethics; but I am asking God to grant me a full working knowledge of everything, so that it can be at His disposal, even for KIA (Kingdom Intelligence Agency) adaptation.

---

27.   Drive-in cinema on the beach, separated from Kingston Harbour only by the Palisadoes peninsula.

I have a few pounds of winter and motorist fat to lose, so I bought myself the first pair of 'track shoes' I've bought since coming here, to re-work some walking into my routine ... By the way, parking is not an incidental expense here; it can be major. So, many motorists use the 'Park 'n Ride' facility provided by the bus company, where they only drive to the bus station, park at a subsidised rate in a huge parking lot there, and hop onto the bus. Then, there is the 'Transit-way,' a network of bus-only roads, which allows express routes to get people to major centres in no time. Some people use bicycles instead of cars in good weather, and many of the buses also have a rack on the front, where they can stash the bicycle till they get off the bus. Only in very new parts of the city do you actually need a car after the winter months, if you live a *moderate*, organised life ...

Things have been a bit unstable at the bank, as the branch is being re-vamped in line with some new ... human resource strategies. (Actually, they are trying to replace as many people with computerisation as possible, over the next few years.) Anyway, we all had to reapply for new positions with altered job descriptions. Nevertheless, in the midst of all that, I insisted on taking two days off twice, to study in peace for exams. Between the change of temperature, spring pollen flying and the waves of anxiety, I have had a bit of chest tightness lately. There was also some briefly exacerbated PMS ☺, but I have survived, and so has Mike.

Praise the Lord; we have been able to secure a commitment of sponsorship for Mission School, of over $3,000 Canadian in the 2001/2002 school year, from Church # 3. Any of you brethren who can get support from new sources for the school, please keep trying, as the need is great. And pray for G, M, and the ministry, for success in finding the Lord's will together, and pursuing it with utmost priority.

My hair is now shoulder length, which is a nice change. Deb relaxes and clips it for me, and the greying has slowed down. I really take care of it—can you imagine? Totally un-Evangeline-like! But it goes to show, I am not really a workaholic at heart. Perhaps, the moment I have (a more stressful) life to deal with again for any length of time, the hair will go the way of all flesh.

Deb is preparing for the final Grade 13 exams, after which she should have the six OAC's required for university matriculation. (Ontario Academic Credits—supposedly the equivalent of A Levels, but you do them in modular form, spreading them over the four semesters of Grades 12 and 13. Of course, you must have the prerequisite courses to do the OAC's, so some still end up doing most toward the end of Grade 13.) Deb already has three, and Joe has one. She is awaiting admission offers from three universities, which should come this month, as the high schools feed the results of applicants directly to the universities. She expects to do the Bachelor of Nursing degree, which is being heavily promoted by the government now, because Canada is short of nurses. The US is recruiting Canadian nurses as fast as Canada has been training them, and of course, the US pays more. So, Canada will have to match the salary lure, as well as increase the undergraduate recruitment.

Joe has been working at a trendy shoe store ... for the past couple of weeks. If all goes well, he could remain with them until he can get something more in line with his career goals. Some students land really good jobs that accommodate them through high school and university, with their changing schedules of availability. (Some older students) are placed in career-goal-related jobs through the 'co-op' system ... where they work part time for three purposes: pay, job experience, and credits toward their degree. Of course, (one source of) Canada's ... cheap labour is students, but in return, some employers treat them really well, and they learn life skills as well as job skills this way.

Deb is a hit with the local YMCA, for which she works at two of their outlets. She supervises children's programs, organises birthday parties, etc. It's hectic work, but she enjoys the children, and is learning smart money management as she looks forward to helping herself through university ... The foot she damaged in the winter fall is now much better, with recent treatment from an orthopaedic specialist. He said the lingering condition was tendonitis, and prescribed anti-inflammatory medication and new arch supports.

I think that's all from me for now. I'm sure your eyes have had it with my epistle. By the way, check out the writer's comment after 13 chapters of Hebrews, (verse22): "I have written you only a short letter." He must have drawn a ☺ that was not transcribed!
Love and blessings to you and yours,
Evangeline

Thursday, September 20, 2001, 4 a.m.

Letter drafted in Jamaica, to be sent as email attachment to Home Church brethren, (but never sent due to difficulty with email access in Mountain Village, where I was visiting for a month to serve as Acting Principal at Mission School.)

Dear Brethren,

I have to testify of the goodness of the Lord. I have been fighting a cold for the past few days—ears, nose, throat, chest, and all the passages feeling more and more affected up to a few minutes ago. All I have used were some Vicks lozenges on Tuesday night. Yesterday, I forgot them at home, so they were no help.

I woke up at minutes to 4 this morning, to pray and get off to an early start, as I have some personal stuff to do before school stuff. But when I tried to swallow, it was horrendous. I tried a few times. So I thought, "My God! Is this 'strep throat' or something? Should I have G look at it today and medicate me?"

Then, the Holy Spirit decided to give me an object lesson to reinforce something I have been learning about, called the 'speedy justice of God.' The thought came to me to speak to my throat in Jesus' name. Ari was sleeping next to me, so I just whispered, "In the name of Jesus Christ, I command this throat to be healed." Then, I swallowed again, and—stupid me—I just couldn't believe the difference! Wow—I used to speak to headaches and this would happen, but never to anything so absolutely 'un-psychosomatic' as a bad sore throat. So, I'm here sharing this with you, and swallowing just for fun! Praise the Lord!

The 'speedy justice of God' is a self-explanatory phrase, but what I have been learning is that it follows and attends the 24/7 practice of praise, worship, intercession, and application of the Word. Since I stepped onto Air Canada on September 1, I have been on a partial fast, both for Mission School and for success in other things I want to achieve. I have also been steadfast in an attitude and practice of praise, worship, thanksgiving, speaking of the goodness of the Lord at every opportunity, and trying to demonstrate His love to others. Even some taxi drivers have got a liberal dose from me. "Praise the Lord!" has been a greeting on my lips and a frequent response to the greeting of others, even when sometimes it has sounded out of place. (This is not in the midst of a bed of roses, for in the past week I have had to resist occasional panic over the unyielding problems of Mission School's headship. G, now that I have encouraged her, was the one to encourage me yesterday evening.

I may not be at Home Church on Sunday morning, as I have to do something for Ari that I may not be able to do at another time, and this will be my last Sunday here. So, I may have little opportunity to share this encouragement with you in person. There are two tapes that I am going to leave with F, with the prayer that they will bless her and others of you. The speakers are not great preachers or teachers, just an intercessor and a music minister sharing on their introduction to a 'new' move of God, dubbed the 'Harp and Bowl Model' of intercession. Much of what North Americans have thus labelled is quite familiar to us; but personally, I have been enlightened by (the) teaching on the rationale, history, structured and consistent application of what has sometimes come naturally to us in the Holy Ghost.

Bless the Lord; and blessings on you too. It's time for work; and the 'speedy justice of God' for Mission School.

Love,

Evangeline

Bibliography

Allen, Reginald. "GG declares himself a reformed sinner." *Sunday Herald*, October 17, 1999, p. 1A.

Anderson, Marcia E. "The Sacrifice of Volunteers." *The Gleaner*, July 4, 2000. (Letters to the Editor.)

Bennett, Louise. *Jamaica Labrish*. Kingston: Sangster's Book Stores Jamaica, 1995.

Boswell, Randy. "A City of Villages." *Ottawa Citizen*, November 30, 1999, p. B1

Byers, Andrew R. (Editor). "Living With Snow." *Readers Digest Atlas of Canada*, 1995, p. 18.

Byers, Andrew R. (Editor). "The Nation and the Provinces." *Readers Digest Atlas of Canada*, 1995, pp. 50, 51.

Grant, Gloria. *Flush, in Jesus' Name! ... And Other Stories*. Kingston, Jamaica: Gloria Grant, 1993.

Howe, Judy. *Pre-Algebra Basic Mathematics II, Second Edition*. Pensacola, Florida. A Beka Book, 1983

Ontario Ministry of Education Internet Site, http://www.edu.gov.on.ca./eng/general/elemsec/es_overview.html, accessed August 13, 2002.

Ontario Ministry of the Attorney General Internet Site, http://www.attorneygeneral.jus.gov.on.ca/html/CAD/stats98–99/tab08p02.pdf, accessed August 13, 2002 Statistics Canada's Internet Site, http://statcan.ca/english,Pgdb/People/Population/demo08.htm, accessed August 12, 2002

Statistics Canada's Internet Site, http://statcan.ca/english,Pgdb/People/Population/demo40b.htm, accessed August 12, 2002.

Statistics Canada's Internet Site, http://statcan.ca/english,Pgdb/People/Population/demo42f.htm, accessed August 12, 2002.

Statistics Canada's Internet Site, http://geodepot2.statcan.ca/Diss/Highlights/Page4/Page4_e.cfm, accessed August 12, 2002.

Statistics Canada's Internet Site, http://www.statcan.ca/english/census96/nov4/table7.htm, accessed August 12, 2002.

Statistics Canada's Internet Site, http://statcan.ca/english,Pgdb/People/Population/demo25b.htm, accessed August 12, 2002.

Statistics Canada's Internet Site, http://www.statcan.ca/english/Pgdb/People/Labour/labour07b.htm, accessed August 12, 2002.

Statistics Canada's Internet Site, http://statcan.ca/english/Pgdb/People/Families/families55e.htm, accessed August 13, 2002.

Statistics Canada's Internet Site, http://statcan.ca/english/Pgdb/Economy/Communications/trade18.htm, accessed August 13, 2002.

Statistics Canada's Internet Site, http://www.statcan.ca/english/Pgdb/People/Families/famil10c.htm, accessed August 13, 2002.

Statistics Canada's Internet Site, http://geodepot2.statcan.ca/Diss/Highlights/Page2/Page2_e.cfm, accessed August 12, 2002.

Statistics Canada's Internet Site, http://geodepot2.statcan.ca/Discuss/Highlights/Page9/Page9b_e.cfm, accessed August 12, 2002.

Statistics Canada's Internet Site, http://www.statcan.ca/english/Pgdb/demo42_96f.htm, accessed April 18, 2004

Transport Canada's Internet Site, http://www.tc.gc.ca/mediaroom/speeches/2000/000603e-fcm.htm, accessed April 11, 2004